MARSILIO CLASSICS

Luigi Ballerini and Paolo Barlera
Series Editors

Heinrich Heine

THE HARZ JOURNEY

Bilingual Edition

Translated by CHARLES G. LELAND
Preface by CLAUDIO MAGRIS

Marsilio
New York

Original German Title
Die Harzreise (1826)

Preface copyright © 1994
by Marsilio Editori, Venezia

Of this edition copyright © 1995
by Marsilio Publishers, Corp.
853 Broadway
New York, NY 10003

Distributed in the U.S.A. by
Consortium Book Sales and Distribution
1045 Westgate Drive
Saint Paul, MN 55114

ISBN hc 1-56886-002-1
ISBN pb 1-56886-003-X

CONTENTS

PREFACE

Romanticism is not just an era of great journeys—real and poetical, physical and metaphorical—but also a period in which the journey, in both its structure and nature, undergoes profound changes. There is no single pattern to this romantic journey, but rather, many patterns, each of them nonetheless marking a profound transformation, a definite break with past eras. Romanticism knows travel above all as a philosophical metaphor, albeit one rudely cast down into reality and transfigured into poetry—an odyssey or path through the world in quest of one's identity. Thus the question asked in Novalis's *Heinrich von Ofterdingen,* "Where are you going?" meets with the reply, "Homeward, always homeward." Like Odysseus of old, yet steeled by a philosophical awareness, Novalis's hero plunges into the giddy whirl of things to find, in the end, himself; his journey leads him to discover his own truth, which had glimmered in him at first only like some uncertain, latent power, but which on confrontation with the world achieves a complete identity.

Like Ithaca, every *Heimat,* homeland, birthplace is found, as Ernst Bloch would say, not at the start, not in childhood and the past, but rather at the end of the journey: it is a destination, not a point of departure. In that great travel novel, Hegel's *Phenomenology of Spirit,* the subject takes leave of itself, immerses in the world and thereby comes into its own, into a self quite other than it was initially, just as the Ithaca Ulysses rediscovers on his return takes on its true meaning only at that moment, much different from that of the one he

left behind. Voyaging, in the Romantic era, is a way of keeping the commandment "Know thyself."

The "wayfarer" of Goethe's early years also ventures far and wide, only he moves toward a destination he has basically harbored within him all the while. Nevertheless the voyage begins to bring out his destructive aspects, that element of cruelty which, many years hence, Canetti will see in all travellers, prone as they are to contemplate reality with curiosity, thus, to observe and understand—and somehow, if only passively, to accept—evil rather than battle it. A certain charge of destruction, of uprootedness and betrayal, is always inherent in travel; the voyager not only relativizes values, he also pries himself loose from his original values and so destroys them, as the example of Goethe's wayfarer shows. E.T.A. Hoffman depicted, particularly in *The Devil's Elixirs*, the violent, demonic aspect of the voyage, viewed (ironically enough, against the backdrop of the "voyage to Italy" that had once stood precisely for harmony) as a descent to the underworld and the realm of one's own personality, thus anticipating the doleful, relentless voyages of those nomads and vagabonds who will turn up again in the literature of the European *fin de siècle*.

The very joy, then, implicit in the vagabond's freedom starts to look problematic; Eichenforff's romantic wayfarer happily abandons himself to the joys of the open road, a joy interchangeable with that of singing, his song echoing the hidden one the world is secretly singing; for this very reason he does not travel in order to arrive somewhere and thereby wreck every moment as he presses on toward a fixed goal, wishing he had already reached it and his journey were already over; rather, he travels to pause, to sojourn, to ramble, to stray from all preestablished routes and from all destinations, never to arrive. Yet even this happy wayfarer is assailed by a troubling

thought: he would like, through his journey, to overtake Life, real and essential life, though such a life seems possible only if it is stripped of all concrete historical and social particularity, if it is reduced to a pure, vague flow—and if the traveller is literally good for nothing [a reference Eichendorff's novella, literally "From the Life of a Good-for-Nothing" —trans.] unfit to do anything whatsoever, to fit, in any way, into the productive mechanism of reality, since, in his view, living means only this.

The grand utopia of Wilhelm Meister—that other vagabond-traveller who eventually takes his positive place in the prose of the world—crumbles. In order truly to *be*, the traveller—the individual —must be *nothing* specific or else he cannot truly be; life becomes a hindrance, an obstacle to itself, trapped in a discontent that will erupt, magnificent and corrosive, in the European literature and philosophy of the *fin de siècle*, from Jacobsen to Goncharov, from Ibsen to Michelstaedter, to cite but a few examples.

Romanticism is a learned, indeed erudite age, but the great prototype of refined travel geared toward concrete discovery of the world, as practiced and perfected in Englightenment tradition, seems almost irreparably lost now—as though one no longer traveled for edification and education, but rather to lose oneself, to erase one's traces, to camouflage oneself amid the busy hum of things. From the promotional, edifying Grand Tour, the premise for a positive social and cultural entrée into reality, travel is transformed or at least starts to be transformed, into flight or regression, at any rate an experience of the uncertainty of one's identity.

Romanticism takes up—though altering its meaning—the tradition of the learned, connoisseur's Tour of the eighteenth century. Heine too—indeed, Heine above all—does this by referring to such precedents as Jean Paul and Sterne. Sterne's

example stands basically for two things: the sentimental journey and the learned journey, fused and inextricably joined in
irony. Making "a sentimental journey" means concentrating
attention not only, and not so much, on the great monuments
and moments of cultural history, but above all on those little
details, seemingly irrelevant, that, like fitful lightning flashes,
bring sudden transparency to an otherwise inaccessible univer-
sality. Taverns, the transient colors of a sky or an evening, the
smile on a face, chatter or squabbling caught by chance on the
street, become the narrow openings through which to gain a
fleeting glance at that All, that Cosmos, otherwise screened
from sense, or presumptuously falsified in being rendered
monumentally, or by direct apprehension.

Grandeur and history can be grasped only in the tender,
palpitant frailty of existence, in the nuances of feeling, in the
precariousness of the everyday; irony signifies awareness of
the finitude of all reality—starting with that of the speaker,
writer, traveller himself—in relation to the infinite. Irony
thus becomes a lucid, yet tender and compassionate way to
love and reconcile oneself to the finitude and misery of
human existence.

Learned travel means that this transpires not only—or no
longer—in a free encounter between the wayfarer's soul and
the purity of nature, as it did for Eichendorff, but rather that
the journey or contact with nature moves through a complex,
endless series of mediations, reflections, schemes, ruses,
digressions. Nature, which the romantic soul ardently wishes
to reach directly, is inaccessible in its immediacy. The one
route toward that Nature passes through reflection, via dusty
tomes that strive to give utterance to life and while failing in
that mission, express its essence by their very testimony of
their failure and its unattainability; it passes through dusty,
erudite scribblings, inn signs, Latin tombstone inscriptions,

writings on the doors of taverns or churches, codicils of rules
and regulations—the whole system, that is, of laws, norms,
rules and regulations that seek to entrap life.

Stale and lifeless as this bookish culture may seem, it is precisely thanks to it that we perceive that nostalgia for real life a
falsely naive lingering romanticism deludes itself into thinking
it can easily attain, shutting itself out from everything in the
process; whereas Heine, great poet that he is, manages to reach
this real life solely by setting out on a perilously papery odyssey.
In this sense, the presence of the law and its metaphorical
valence play a central role in both the journey and its poetical
rendering. As one scholar-critic has noted, legal reflection
plays a fundamental part in Heine's poetics, leading him from
a youthful fealty to German "choral poetry" (that is, from the
illusion that there is something intrinsically poetic about the
stratified, centuries-old diversity of German society) to the
intuition of a new poetry that can arise only through refusing
Germany's woes and insufficiencies and assuming a progres-
sive, Napoleonic conception of life and history.

Law, then, in Heine's journey, fulfills an essential poetic
function. It becomes the metaphor, the very language, of poetry.
Law expresses at once the classifying of life in all its unlawful-
ness anad irregularity, and the anarchic force of this vital irregularity, which revolts against all order, but reveals its own
vibrant tension only in contrast to such classifying. The law,
which Salvatore Satta has defined as a thing "as terrible as
life," arises out of an intuition of the ineluctable conflict
implicit in existence and out of a desire to bring order to it not
only by the constraints of laws and sanctions, but also by clas-
sically-based intellectual knowledge.

Law, for Heine, becomes a kind of poetic language: that of
the paper map that culture and society has spread—and cannot help but spread—over the diversity of life, of people and

things, of traditions, places. The traveller buries himself in this
literary-juridical map of reality, but at times worms his way
into some cranny where he can reencounter nature, the poetry
of the heart, the enchantment of life's pure flow—an enchantment which can only contrast with the short-circuit that binds
him to the dusty yet oddly moving conceptual architecture of
pandects, paragraphs, sentences, words.

Heine's journey, so full of love for existence and for nature,
winds its way between cartography and life; between the map
covering the world with the quirky, meticulous, fastidious variety juridical precision vouchsafes it, and the bumpy, motley,
uneven surface of life itself that map covers. In this sense
Heine does create a model journey, or in any case freshly
reworks the consummate model Sterne bequeathed him; the
ironic, erudite journey, impossible without philological and
juridical precision, which tenderly approaches life well aware
it will abscond or take flight on approach. And should life
assume the guise of Old Germany, then that country's "good
old law," in all its "splendor and misery" becomes a language
all the more necessary as the means to departure and descent
to the roots of one's own world and one's persona. *Jus*, Law,
with its tortuous terminology, so fondly mocked by the poet, is
like a rough and crumpled paper flower that nods yearningly
to those other flowers, the ones that are living (but oh! how
briefly) out there in the meadow — those flowers Heine, and
others with him, wants to celebrate in song.

Claudio Magris

translated by David Jacobson

THE AUTHOR AND HIS WORK

1797: Heinrich Heine is born in Düsseldorf on 13 December, to Jewish parents: his mother, Betty van Geldern, is descended from a respected family of Rhineland scholars and bankers; his father, Samson, a textile merchant, comes from Hannover. The eldest child, he will have a sister and two brothers.

1798: In February "Harry" is circumcised and officially registered among the Jewish community.

1804: In August he enter the school in a former Franciscan convent, while receiving his religious education at the private Hebrew school of Hein Herz Rintelsohn.

1806: Joachim Murat, named "Grand Duke of Berg," installs himself in Dsseldorf with French troops. Billetted in the Heine house is a drum major: the inspiration for the figure Le Grand in *Ideen. Das Buch Le Grand* [*Ideas: The Book of Le Grand*, 1827].

1807: Heine attends the *Gymnasium* of the former Franciscan convent.

1811: He views Napoleon passing on horseback in the Hofgarten.

1814: He gets to know his cousin Amalie, the daughter of his father's brother Salomon, a very wealthy banker in Hamburg. His parents, in financial straits, want to set their son up in business.

1815: In September he accompanies his father to the Frankfurt Fair, discovers the sad reality of the city's ghetto, and meets Börne.

1816: In Hamburg he starts a business apprenticeship under his uncle Salomon. His hopes to obtain his cousin's love go unrequited.

1817: He publishes his first poems under a pseudonym.

1818: His uncle sets him up in a shop handling English fabric; when it fails, Solomon agrees to pay for his legal studies.

1819: In December, Heine enrolls at the University of Bonn: in addition to his law courses, he attends the lectures of A.W. Schlegel (on German metrics and the *Nibelungenlied*) and E.M. Arndt (on Tacitus' *Germania*). He is active in one of the liberal-national students fraternities: the *Burschenschaft Allgemeinheit*.

1820: Schlegel offers him valuable advice on his poems. In October he enrolls at Göttingen, where he is suspended for six months by the academic senate for participating in a duel.

1821: From April on, he studies in Berlin: he is drawn to the courses in law (Savigny analyzing the *Pandects*), philosophy (Hegel and Schleiermacher), and philology (Böck, Bopp). His social life burgeons as well: in May begins his long friendship with Rahel and Karl August Varnhagen von Ense; soon after he mingles with Chamisso, Fichte, Hegel, Alexander von Humboldt, Fouqué, Alexis, Grabbe. In December his small poetry volume, *Gedichte*, appears.

1822: His first journalistic correspondences, the *Briefe aus Berlin* [*Letters from Berlin*]. He participates with Zunz and Moser in the "Verein," the Jewish cultural association presided over by the Hegelian jurist Gans. In September he visits Poland (*Über Polen*, [*On Poland*], 1823).

1823: In April he publishes in one volume his two and only tragedies (*Almansor* and *Ratcliff*) and the *Lyrisches Intermezzo* [*Lyric Intermezzo*];

a copy is sent to Goethe (and others to Uhland, Wilhelm Müller, Immermann). In May he joins his parents, who have moved to Lüneberg. In the summer he writes many of the poems of *Heimkehr* [*Homecoming*].

1824: In January, back at Göttingen, he decides to complete his law studies. In September his walking tour of the Harz Mountains takes him to Weimar: there he has a disappointing visit with Goethe, who receives him rather stiffly.

1825: On 28 June Heine is baptised a Protestant (the "entry ticket into European culture"); 25 July: he finishes his degree, under Gustav Hugo. He spends the summer at Norderney, on the North Sea. In Hamburg, he starts to plan a career as a lawyer.

1826: In May the publisher Campe, who will henceforth take on all his works, brings out, in one volume, the *Reisebilder I, Die Harzreise* [*Travel Pictures I, The Harz Journey*].

1827: In April the sequel volume, *Reisebilder II* [*Travel Pictures II*] appears, containing *Ideas: The Book of Le Grand* and the poems of *Nordsee II* [*North Sea II*]. A stay in London produces *Englische Fragmente* [*English Fragments*], 1828. On his return to Hamburg he publishes, in October, the highly successful *Buch der Lieder* [*The Book of Songs*], which changes the order of his earlier poetry collections. In November he goes to Munich, with the idea of working for a new political journal put out by the publisher Cotta.

1828: Travel in Italy: Trento, Verona, Milan, Genoa, Leghorn, Bagni di Lucca, Florence, Venice. He returns to Munich in mid-December. Cotta abandons his plans for the journal and informs Heine that the poet August von Platen has written a vicious attack on him.

1829: He spends much of the year in Berlin, where he regularly visits the Varnhagens, and works on *Reisebilder III* [*Travel Pictures III*], containing the *Journey from Munich to Genoa* and *The Baths of Lucca*, which appear at the end of December, creating a scandal through his fierce rebuttal to Platen.

1830: A summer stay at Helgoland, where he jubilantly celebrates the news of the July Revolution. In October, in Hamburg, he writes the first draft of *Reisebilder IV* [*Travel Pictures IV*] (*The City of Lucca*, 1831).

1831: With no hope now of finding an acceptable position in Germany, he decides to emigrate. On 19 May he arrives in Paris, which opens its salons and intellectuals to him: he meets Bazard, Berlioz, Cherubini, Chopin, Gautier, Lafayette, Liszt, Michelet; he regularly mingles with Princess Belgiojoso, Chevalier, Mendelssohn-Bartoldy, Meyerbeer, James de Rothschild, Thiers, de Vigny, and, later, Hugo, Dumas *père*, Mme D'Agoult, and Sainte-Beuve. He also meets the exiled Börne.

1832: He attends the meetings of the Saint-Simonists. For the Augusta's *Gazette* he reports on the political situation in France: the articles will be collected in 1833 in *Französische Zustände* [*French Circumstances*]. He makes the acquaintance of Balzac.

1833: He meets Alfred de Musset. His disagreements with Börne and the German republicans mount. While informing the Germans on current events in France, he introduces the French to German culture: the articles for "L'Europe littéraire" grow into *Die Romantische Schule* [*The Romantic School*, German editions 1833 and 1835]. In December, together with various journalistic reports on French painters, he publishes *Aus den Memoiren des Herren Schnabelowopski* [*From the Memoirs of Mr. Schnabelowopski*].

1834: In January he focuses his work on *Zur Geschichte der Religion und Philosophie in Deutschland* [*On the History of Religion and Philosophy in Germany*], which will first come out in a French translation, followed by the German original in 1835. In October he meets Crescence Eugenie Mirat—the companion known as "Mathilde," whom, after years of living together, he will marry on 31 August 1841.

1835: He becomes friendly with Bellini. On 10 December a decree of the German federal Diet against the "subversive" group known as Young Germany bans the publications of Heine, Gutzkow, Laube, Mundt, Wienbarg.

1836: In autumn he travels to Provence.

1837: In May, a stay in Brittany. Publication of *Florentinische Nächte* [*Florentine Nights*] and *Elementargeister* [*Elemental Spirits*].

1838: In Paris he publishes *Shakespeares Mädchen und Frauen* [*Shakespeare's Girls and Women*].

1839: In April he gathers notes for his book on Börne (who died in January 1837); Campe will bring out this polemical essay the following year.

1840: In November *Der Rabbi von Bacharach* [*The Rabbi of Bacharach*] appears. New journalistic reporting from Paris, collected in 1854 under the title *Lutetia*.

1841: In June, a vacation in the Pyranees.

1843: In October his first trip back to Germany since exile: he arrives in Hamburg via Brussels, Münster, Osnabrck. In December he is back again in Paris, where he meets Marx.

1844: In "Vorwärts," the socialist journal, he publishes the poem *Die Weber* [*The Weavers*], inspired by the revolt in Silesia. In July, his second trip to Germany, with Mathilde. In September the volume *Neue Gedichte* [*New Poems*] appears, containing *Deutschland. Ein Wintermärchen* [*Germany, A Winter's Tale*], later reprinted in "Vorwärts." On 23 December his uncle Solomon dies; a long family legal battle ensues.

1847: In January appears the poem *Atta Troll. Ein Sommernachstraum* [*Atta Troll, A Summer Night's Dream*], a satire on the tendentious poets of the day.

1848: In February he visits a clinic for tests, after worrisome signs of paresis (partial motor paralysis). When the Febuary Revolution erupts, Heine is present at the street fighting. In mid-May, in the Louvre,

before the statue of the Venus de Milo, he suffers a decisive collapse: for the rest of his days paralysis will confine him to his "mattress tomb."

1851: Despite his illness, he continues to write, publishing in mid-October the poems of *Romanzero* and the libretto for *Der Doktor Faust.*

1854: Publication of *Vermischte Schriften* [*Miscellaneous Writings*], including, among other works: his *Geständnisse* [*Confessions*], *Die Götter im Exil* [*The Gods in Exile*], *Die Göttin Diana* [*The Goddess Diana*]. He organizes the edition of his complete works.

1855: He is cheered by the constant friendship of the admirer known as "la Mouche."

1856: Heine dies the morning of 17 February; on the 20th he is buried in Montmartre cemetery.

Maria Carolina Foi

translated by David Jacobson

NOTE TO THE TEXT

The German text (*Die Harzreise*) is taken from the edition of Heinrich Heine's complete works: *Sämtliche Schriften*, Klaus Briegleb ed., vol. 3, Frankfurt-Berlin-Wien, Ullstein, 1981, pp. 97-166. The choice of this edition, which follows those by Ernst Elster (Leipzig, 1887–90) and by Oskar Walzel (Leipzig, 1910–20), is largely due to its consideration of Heine's own indications (particularly regarding punctuation) in his last authorized version.

The English traslation by Charles G. Leland is taken from his *Pictures of Travel* (1855, pp. 1-61), which was probably based on an earlier version of *Die Harzreise* than the one presented here. (For the very few variants, see notes 22 and 72). First published when Heine was still alive, Leland's version has the merit of gracefully capturing the spirit of the time and thus rendering the richness of the original's irony and allusions.

An American journalist and humorist, C.G. Leland (1824–1903) spent most of his later career in London (1869–79) and Florence (after 1884). Besides his distinguished translations (which were to include Heine's complete writings), Leland authored of several works, notably among them *Meister Karl's Sketch-Book* (1855) and *Hans Breitmann's Party* (1957), first contributed to *Graham's Magazine* and later collected in *The Breitmann's Ballads* (1871)

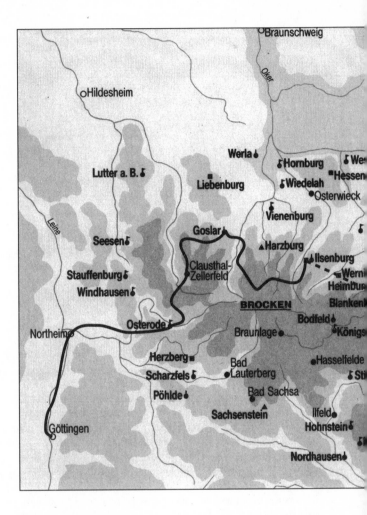

The continuous line denotes Heine's itinerary through the Harz region. The dotted line denotes Heine's route back to Göttingen, through the Weimar region.

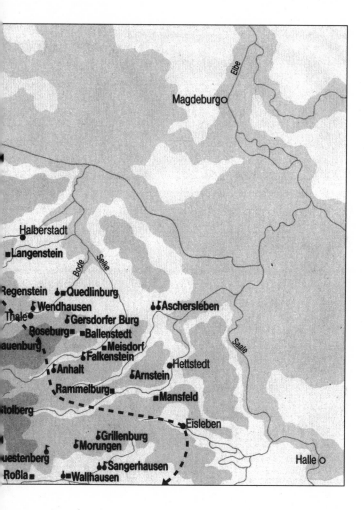

Magdeburg

Elbe

Halberstadt
Langenstein
Regenstein Quedlinburg
Wendhausen
Thale Gersdorfer Burg
Boseburg Ballenstedt
auenburg Meisdorf
Falkenstein
Anhalt Arnstein Hettstedt
Rammelburg
Mansfeld
tolberg
Eisleben
Grillenburg
Morungen
uestenberg Sangerhausen
Roßla Wallhausen Halle

Bode Selke

Saale

xxiii

THE HARZ JOURNEY

DIE HARZREISE

DIE HARZREISE

Nichts ist dauernd, als der Wechsel; nichts beständig, als der Tod. Jeder Schlag des Herzens schlägt uns eine Wunde, und das Leben wäre ein ewiges Verbluten, wenn nicht die Dichtkunst wäre. Sie gewährt uns, was uns die Natur versagt: eine goldene Zeit, die nicht rostet, einen Frühling, der nicht abblüht, wolkenloses Glück und ewige Jugend. *Börne.*

Schwarze Röcke, seidne Strümpfe,
Weiße, höfliche Manschetten,
Sanfte Reden, Embrassieren –
Ach, wenn sie nur Herzen hätten!

Herzen in der Brust, und Liebe,
Warme Liebe in dem Herzen –
Ach, mich tötet ihr Gesinge
Von erlognen Liebesschmerzen.

Auf die Berge will ich steigen,
Wo die frommen Hütten stehen,
Wo die Brust sich frei erschließet,
Und die freien Lüfte wehen.

Auf die Berge will ich steigen,
Wo die dunkeln Tannen ragen,
Bäche rauschen, Vögel singen,
Und die stolzen Wolken jagen.

Lebet wohl, ihr glatten Säle,
Glatte Herren! Glatte Frauen!
Auf die Berge will ich steigen,
Lachend auf Euch niederschauen.

THE HARZ JOURNEY

"Nothing is permanent but change, nothing constant but death. Every pulsation of the heart inflicts a wound, and life would be an endless bleeding, were it not for Poetry. She secures to us what Nature would deny; a golden age without rust, a spring which never fades, cloudless prosperity and eternal youth."

Börne[1]

Black dress coats and silken stockings,[2]
Snowy ruffles frilled with art,
Gentle speeches and embraces—
Oh, if they but held a heart!

Held a heart within their bosom,
Warmed by love which truly glows;
Ah—I'm wearied with their chanting
Of imagined lover's woes!

I will climb upon the mountains
Where the quiet cabin stands,
Where the wind blows freely o'er us,
Where the heart at ease expands.

I will climb upon the mountains
Where the dark green fir-trees grow;
Brooks are rustling, birds are singing,
And the wild clouds headlong go.

Then farewell, ye polished ladies,
Polished men, and polished hall!
I will climb upon the mountain,
Smiling down upon you all.

3

Die Stadt Göttingen, berühmt durch ihre Würste und Universität, gehört dem Könige von Hannover, und enthält 999 Feuerstellen, diverse Kirchen, eine Entbindungsanstalt, eine Sternwarte, einen Karzer, eine Bibliothek und einen Ratskeller, wo das Bier sehr gut ist. Der vorbeifließende Bach heißt »die Leine« und dient des Sommers zum Baden; das Wasser ist sehr kalt und an einigen Orten so breit, daß Lüder wirklich einen großen Anlauf nehmen mußte, als er hinüber sprang. Die Stadt selbst ist schön, und gefällt einem am besten, wenn man sie mit dem Rücken ansieht. Sie muß schon sehr lange stehen; denn ich erinnere mich, als ich vor fünf Jahren dort immatrikuliert und bald darauf konsiliiert wurde, hatte sie schon dasselbe graue, altkluge Ansehen, und war schon vollständig eingerichtet mit Schnurren, Pudeln, Dissertationen, Teedansants, Wäscherinnen, Kompendien, Taubenbraten, Guelfenorden, Promotionskutschen, Pfeifenköpfen, Hofräten, Justizräten, Relegationsräten, Profaxen und anderen Faxen. Einige behaupten sogar, die Stadt sei zur Zeit der Völkerwanderung erbaut worden, jeder deutsche Stamm habe damals ein ungebundenes Exemplar seiner Mitglieder darin zurückgelassen, und davon stammten all die Vandalen, Friesen, Schwaben, Teutonen, Sachsen, Thüringer usw., die noch heut zu Tage in Göttingen, hordenweis, und geschieden durch Farben der Mützen und der Pfeifenquäste, über die Weenderstraße einherziehen, auf den blutigen Walstätten der Rasenmühle, des Ritschenkrugs und Bovdens sich ewig unter einander herumschlagen, in Sitten und Gebräuchen noch immer wie zur Zeit der Völkerwanderung dahinleben, und teils durch ihre Duces, welche Haupthähne heißen, teils durch ihr uraltes Gesetzbuch, welches Comment heißt und in den legibus barbarorum eine Stelle verdient, regiert werden.

Im allgemeinen werden die Bewohner Göttingens eingeteilt in Studenten, Professoren, Philister und Vieh; welche vier Stände doch nichts weniger als streng geschieden sind. Der Viehstand ist der bedeutendste. Die Namen aller Studenten und

The town of Göttingen, celebrated for its sausages and University,[3] belongs to the King of Hannover, and contains nine hundred and ninety-nine dwellings, divers churches, a lying-in asylum, an observatory, a prison, a library, and a "council-cellar," where the beer is excellent. The stream which flows by the town is termed "the Leine," and is used in summer for bathing, its waters being very cold, and in more than one place so broad, that Lüder was obliged to take quite a run ere he could leap across.[4] The town itself is beautiful, and pleases most when looked at backwards. It must be very ancient, for I well remember that five years ago, when I was there matriculated (and shortly after "summoned"), it had already the same gray, old-fashioned, wise look, and was fully furnished with beggars, beadles, dissertations, tea-parties with a little dancing, washerwomen, compendiums, roasted pigeons, Guelfic orders, professors ordinary and extraordinary, pipe heads, court-counselors, and law-counselors.[5] Many even assert that at the time of the great migration of races, every German tribe left a badly corrected proof of its existence in the town, in the person of one of its members, and that from these descended all the Vandals, Frisians, Suabians, Teutons, Saxons, Thuringians, and others who at the present day abound in Göttingen, where, separately distinguished by the color of their caps and pipe tassels, they may be seen straying singly or in hordes along the Weender Street.[6] They still fight their battles on the bloody arena of the Rasenmill, Ritschenkrug, and Bovden,[7] still preserve the mode of life peculiar to their savage ancestors, and are still governed partly by their Duces, whom they call "chief cocks," and partly by their primevally ancient lawbook, known as the *Comment,* which fully deserves a place among the *legibus barbarorum.*

The inhabitants of Göttingen are generally and socially divided into Students, Professors, Philistines, and Cattle, the points of

aller ordentlichen und unordentlichen Professoren hier herzu-
zählen, wäre zu weitläufig; auch sind mir in diesem Augenblick
nicht alle Studentennamen im Gedächtnisse, und unter den
Professoren sind manche, die noch gar keinen Namen haben.
Die Zahl der Göttinger Philister muß sehr groß sein, wie Sand,
oder besser gesagt, wie Kot am Meer; wahrlich, wenn ich sie
des Morgens, mit ihren schmutzigen Gesichtern und weißen
Rechnungen, vor den Pforten des akademischen Gerichtes auf-
gepflanzt sah, so mochte ich kaum begreifen, wie Gott nur so
viel Lumpenpack erschaffen konnte.

Ausführlicheres über die Stadt Göttingen läßt sich sehr bequem nachlesen in der Topographie derselben von K. F. H. Marx.
Obzwar ich gegen den Verfasser, der mein Arzt war und mir
viel Liebes erzeigte, die heiligsten Verpflichtungen hege, so
kann ich doch sein Werk nicht unbedingt empfehlen, und ich
muß tadeln, daß er jener falschen Meinung, als hätten die Göttingerinnen allzugroße Füße, nicht streng genug widerspricht.
Ja, ich habe mich sogar seit Jahr und Tag mit einer ernsten Wider-
legung dieser Meinung beschäftigt, ich habe deshalb verglei-
chende Anatomie gehört, die seltensten Werke auf der Bibliothek exzerpiert, auf der Weenderstraße stundenlang die Füße
der vorübergehenden Damen studiert, und in der grundgelehr-
ten Abhandlung, so die Resultate dieser Studien enthalten wird,
spreche ich 1^0 von den Füßen überhaupt, 2^0 von den Füßen bei
den Alten, 3^0 von den Füßen der Elefanten, 4^0 von den Füßen
der Göttingerinnen, 5^0 stelle ich alles zusammen, was über diese
Füße auf Ullrichs Garten schon gesagt worden, 6^0 betrachte ich
diese Füße in ihrem Zusammenhang, und verbreite mich bei
dieser Gelegenheit auch über Waden, Knie usw., und endlich
7^0, wenn ich nur so großes Papier auftreiben kann, füge ich
noch hinzu einige Kupfertafeln mit dem Faksimile göttingi-
scher Damenfüße.

Es war noch sehr früh, als ich Göttingen verließ, und der
gelehrte ** lag gewiß noch im Bette und träumte wie gewöhn-

difference between these castes being by no means strictly defined. The cattle class is the most important. I might be accused of prolixity should I here enumerate the names of all the students and of all the regular and irregular professors;[8] besides, I do not just at present distinctly remember the appellations of all the former gentlemen, while among the professors are many who as yet have no name at all. The number of the Göttingen Philistines must be as numerous as the sands (or more correctly speaking, as the mud) of the sea; indeed, when I beheld them of a morning, with their dirty faces and clean bills, planted before the gate of the collegiate court of justice, I wondered greatly that such an innumerable pack of rascals should ever have been created.

More accurate information of the town of Göttingen may be very conveniently obtained from its *Topography,* by K.F.H. Marx.[9] Though entertaining the most sacred regard for its author, who was my physician, and manifested for me much esteem, still I cannot pass by his work with altogether unconditional praise, inasmuch as he has not with sufficient zeal combated the erroneous opinions that the ladies of Göttingen have not enormous feet. On this point I speak authoritatively, having for many years been earnestly occupied with a refutation of this opinion. To confirm my views I have not only studied comparative anatomy and made copious extracts from the rarest works in the library, but have also watched for hours, in the Weender Street, the feet of the ladies as they walked by. In the fundamentally erudite treatise which forms the result of these studies, I speak firstly, of feet, in general; secondly, of the feet of antiquity; thirdly, of elephants' feet; fourthly, of the feet of the Göttingen ladies; fifthly, I collect all that was ever said in Ulrich's Garden[10] on the subject of female feet. Sixthly, I regard feet in their connection with each other, availing myself of the opportunity to extend my observation to ankles, calves, knees, etc., and finally and seventhly, if I can manage

lich: er wandle in einem schönen Garten, auf dessen Beeten lauter weiße, mit Zitaten beschriebene Papierchen wachsen, die im Sonnenlichte lieblich glänzen, und von denen er hier und da mehrere pflückt, und mühsam in ein neues Beet verpflanzt, während die Nachtigallen mit ihren süßesten Tönen sein altes Herz erfreuen.

Vor dem Weender Tore begegneten mir zwei eingeborne kleine Schulknaben, wovon der eine zum andern sagte: »Mit dem Theodor will ich gar nicht mehr umgehen, er ist ein Lumpenkerl, denn gestern wußte er nicht mal, wie der Genitiv von Mensa heißt.« So unbedeutend diese Worte klingen, so muß ich sie doch wieder erzählen, ja, ich möchte sie als Stadt-Motto gleich auf das Tor schreiben lassen; denn die Jungen piepsen, wie die Alten pfeifen, und jene Worte bezeichnen ganz den engen, trocknen Notizenstolz der hochgelahrten Georgia Augusta.

Auf der Chaussee wehte frische Morgenluft, und die Vögel sangen gar freudig, und auch mir wurde allmählig wieder frisch und freudig zu Mute. Eine solche Erquickung tat Not. Ich war die letzte Zeit nicht aus dem Pandektenstall herausgekommen, römische Kasuisten hatten mir den Geist wie mit einem grauen Spinnweb überzogen, mein Herz war wie eingeklemmt zwischen den eisernen Paragraphen selbstsüchtiger Rechtssysteme, beständig klang es mir noch in den Ohren wie »Tribonian, Justinian, Hermogenian und Dummerjahn«, und ein zärtliches Liebespaar, das unter einem Baum saß, hielt ich gar für eine Corpusjuris-Ausgabe mit verschlungenen Händen. Auf der Landstraße fing es an, lebendig zu werden. Milchmädchen zogen vorüber; auch Eseltreiber mit ihren grauen Zöglingen. Hinter Weende begegneten mir der Schäfer und Doris. Dieses ist nicht das idyllische Paar, wovon Geßner singt, sondern es sind wohlbestallte Universitätspedelle, die wachsam aufpassen müssen, daß sich keine Studenten in Bovden duellieren, und daß keine neue Ideen, die noch immer einige Dezen-

to hunt up sheets of paper of sufficient size, I will present my readers with some copperplate facsimiles of the feet of the fair dames of Göttingen.

It was as yet very early in the morning when I left Göttingen, and the learned **[11] beyond doubt still lay in bed, dreaming that he wandered in a fair garden, amid the beds of which grew innumerable white papers written over with citations. On these the sun shone cheerily, and he plucked them and planted them in new beds while the sweetest songs of the nightingales rejoiced his old heart.

Before the Weender Gate, I met two native and diminutive schoolboys, one of whom was saying to the other, "I don't intend to keep company any more with Theodore, he is a low little blackguard, for yesterday he didn't even know the genitive of *mensa*." Insignificant as these words may appear, I still regard them as entitled to record—nay, I would even write them as town motto on the gate of Göttingen, for the young birds pipe as the old ones sing, and the expression accurately indicates the narrow-minded academic pride so characteristic of the highly learned Georgia Augusta.

Fresh morning air blew over the road, the birds sang cheerily, and little by little, with the breeze and the birds, my mind also became fresh and cheerful. Such a refreshment was needed for one who had long been imprisoned in a stall of legal lore. Roman casuists had covered my soul with gray cobwebs, my heart was cemented firmly between the iron paragraphs of selfish systems of jurisprudence,[12] there was an endless ringing in my cars of such sounds as "Tribonian, Justinian, Hermogenian,[13] and Blockheadian," and a sentimental brace of lovers seated under a tree appeared to me like an edition of the "Corpus Juris" with closed clasps.[14] The road began to wear a more lively appearance. Milkmaids occasionally passed, as did also donkey drivers with

nien vor Göttingen Quarantäne halten müssen, von einem spe-
kulierenden Privatdozenten eingeschmuggelt werden. Schäfer
grüßte mich sehr kollegialisch; denn er ist ebenfalls Schriftsteller, und hat meiner in seinen halbjährigen Schriften oft er-
wähnt; wie er mich denn auch außerdem oft zitiert hat, und,
wenn er mich nicht zu Hause fand, immer so gütig war, die
Zitation mit Kreide auf meine Stubentür zu schreiben. Dann
und wann rollte auch ein Einspänner vorüber, wohlbepackt mit
Studenten, die für die Ferienzeit, oder auch für immer weg-
reisten. In solch einer Universitätsstadt ist ein beständiges Kommen und Abgehen, alle drei Jahre findet man dort eine neue
Studentengeneration, das ist ein ewiger Menschenstrom, wo
eine Semesterwelle die andere fortdrängt, und nur die alten
Professoren bleiben stehen in dieser allgemeinen Bewegung,
unerschütterlich fest, gleich den Pyramiden Ägyptens – nur
daß in diesen Universitätspyramiden keine Weisheit verborgen
ist.

Aus den Myrtenlauben bei Rauschenwasser sah ich zwei hoff-
nungsvolle Jünglinge hervorreiten. Ein Weibsbild, das dort sein
horizontales Handwerk treibt, gab ihnen bis auf die Landstraße
das Geleit, klätschelte mit geübter Hand die mageren Schenkel
der Pferde, lachte laut auf, als der eine Reuter ihr hinten, auf
die breite Spontaneität einige Galanterien mit der Peitsche über-
langte, und schob sich alsdann gen Bovden. Die Jünglinge aber
jagten nach Nörten, und johlten gar geistreich, und sangen gar
lieblich das Rossinische Lied:»Trink Bier, liebe, liebe Liese!«
Diese Töne hörte ich noch lange in der Ferne; doch die holden
Sänger selbst verlor ich bald völlig aus dem Gesichte, sintemal
sie ihre Pferde, die im Grunde einen deutsch langsamen Charakter zu haben schienen, gar entsetzlich anspornten und vorwärts-
peitschten. Nirgends wird die Pferdeschinderei stärker ge-
trieben als in Göttingen, und oft, wenn ich sah, wie solch eine
schweißtriefende, lahme Kracke, für das bißchen Lebensfutter,
von unsern Rauschenwasserrittern abgequält ward, oder wohl

their gray pupils. Beyond Weender, I met the Shepherd and Doris.[15] This is not the idyllic pair sung by Gessner, but the well-matched University beadles whose duty it is to keep watch and ward, so that no students fight duels in Bovden, and above all that no new ideas (such as are generally obliged to maintain a decennial quarantine before Göttingen) are smuggled in by speculative private teachers. Shepherd greeted me very collegially and congenially, for he too is an author, who has frequently mentioned my name in his semiannual writings. In addition to this, I may mention that when, as was frequently the case, he came to summon me before the University court and found me not at home, he was always kind enough to write the citation with chalk upon my chamber door. Occasionally a one-horse vehicle rolled along, well packed with students, who traveled away for the vacation—or forever. In such a university town, there is an endless coming and going. Every three years beholds a new student generation, forming an incessant human tide, where one vacation wave washes along its predecessor, and only the old professors remain upright in the general flood, immovable as the Pyramids of Egypt. Unlike their oriental contemporaries, no tradition declares that in them treasures of wisdom are buried.

From amid the myrtle leaves, by Rauschenwasser, I saw two hopeful youths appear. A female, who there carried on her business, accompanied them as far as the highway, clapped with a practised hand the meager legs of the horses, laughed aloud, as one of the cavaliers, inspired with a very peculiar spirit of gallantry, gave her a cut behind with his whip, and traveled off for Bovden. The youths, however, rattled along towards Nörten, trilling in a highly intelligent manner, and singing the Rossinian lay of "Drink beer, pretty, pretty Liza!"[16] These sounds I continued to hear when far in the distance, and after I had long lost sight of the amiable vocalists, as their horses, which appeared to be gifted

gar einen ganzen Wagen voll Studenten fortziehen mußte, so dachte ich auch: »O du armes Tier, gewiß haben deine Voreltern im Paradiese verbotenen Hafer gefressen!« Im Wirtshause zu Nörten traf ich die beiden Jünglinge wieder. Der eine verzehrte einen Heringsalat, und der andere unterhielt sich mit der gelbledernen Magd, Fusia Canina, auch Trittvogel genannt. Er sagte ihr einige Anständigkeiten, und am Ende wurden sie Hand-gemein. Um meinen Ranzen zu erleichtern, nahm ich die eingepackten blauen Hosen, die in geschichtlicher Hinsicht sehr merkwürdig sind, wieder heraus und schenkte sie dem kleinen Kellner, den man Kolibri nennt. Die Bussenia, die alte Wirtin, brachte mir unterdessen ein Butterbrot, und beklagte sich, daß ich sie jetzt so selten besuche; denn sie liebt mich sehr.

Hinter Nörten stand die Sonne hoch und glänzend am Himmel. Sie meinte es recht ehrlich mit mir und erwärmte mein Haupt, daß alle unreife Gedanken darin zur Vollreife kamen. Die liebe Wirtshaussonne in Nordheim ist auch nicht zu verachten; ich kehrte hier ein, und fand das Mittagessen schon fertig. Alle Gerichte waren schmackhaft zubereitet, und wollten mir besser behagen, als die abgeschmackten akademischen Gerichte, die salzlosen, ledernen Stockfische mit ihrem alten Kohl, die mir in Göttingen vorgesetzt wurden.

Nachdem ich meinen Magen etwas beschwichtigt hatte, bemerkte ich in derselben Wirtsstube einen Herrn mit zwei Damen, die im Begriff waren abzureisen. Dieser Herr war ganz grün gekleidet, trug sogar eine grüne Brille, die auf seine rote Kupfernase einen Schein wie Grünspan warf, und sah aus wie der König Nebukadnezar in seinen spätern Jahren ausgesehen hat, als er, der Sage nach, gleich einem Tiere des Waldes, nichts als Salat aß. Der Grüne wünschte, daß ich ihm ein Hotel in Göttingen empfehlen möchte, und ich riet ihm, dort von dem ersten besten Studenten das Hotel de Brühbach zu erfragen. Die eine Dame war die Frau Gemahlin, eine gar große, weit-

with characters of extreme German deliberation, were spurred and lashed in a most excruciating style. In no place is the skinning alive of horses carried to such an extent as in Göttingen; and often, when I beheld some lame and sweating back, who, to earn the scraps of fodder which maintained his wretched life, was obliged to endure the torment of some roaring blade, or draw a whole wagon-load of students, I reflected: "Unfortunate beast—most certainly thy first ancestors, in some horse paradise, did eat of forbidden oats."

In the tavern at Nörten I again met my two vocalists. One devoured a herring salad, and the other amused himself with the leathern-complexioned waiting-maid, Fusia Canina,[17] also known as Stepping-bird.[18] He passed from compliments to caresses, until they became finally hand in glove together. To lighten my knapsack, I extracted from it a pair of blue pantaloons, which were somewhat remarkable in a historical point of view,[19] and presented them to the little waiter, whom we called Humming-bird. The old landlady, Bussenia,[20] brought me bread and butter, and greatly lamented that I so seldom visited her, for she loved me dearly.

Beyond Nörten the sun flashed high in heaven. He evidently wished to treat me honorably, and warmed my hear until all the unripe thoughts which it contained came to full growth. The admirable "Sun" tavern, in Nörten, should not be passed over in silence, for it was there that I breakfasted. All the dishes were excellent, and suited me far better than the wearisome, academical courses of saltless, leathery dried fish and cabbage réchauffée, which characterized both our physical and mental pabulum at Göttingen.

After I had somewhat appeased my appetite, I remarked in the same room of the tavern, a gentleman and two ladies, who appeared about to depart on their journey. The cavalier was clad entirely in green, even to his eyes, over which a pair of green

läuftige Dame, ein rotes Quadratmeilen-Gesicht mit Grübchen in den Wangen, die wie Spucknäpfe für Liebesgötter aussahen, ein langfleischig herabhängendes Unterkinn, das eine schlechte Fortsetzung des Gesichtes zu sein schien, und ein hochaufgestapelter Busen, der mit steifen Spitzen und vielzackig festonierten Krägen, wie mit Türmchen und Bastionen umbaut war. Die andere Dame, die Frau Schwester, bildete ganz den Gegensatz der eben beschriebenen. Stammte jene von Pharaos fetten Kühen, so stammte diese von den magern. Das Gesicht nur ein Mund zwischen zwei Ohren, die Brust trostlos öde, wie die Lüneburger Heide; die ganze ausgekochte Gestalt glich einem Freitisch für arme Theologen. Beide Damen fragten mich zu gleicher Zeit: ob im Hotel de Brühbach auch ordentliche Leute logierten. Ich bejahte es mit gutem Gewissen, und als das holde Kleeblatt abfuhr, grüßte ich nochmals zum Fenster hinaus. Der Sonnenwirt lächelte gar schlau und mochte wohl wissen, daß der Karzer von den Studenten in Göttingen Hotel de Brühbach genannt wird.

Hinter Nordheim wird es schon gebirgig und hier und da treten schöne Anhöhen hervor. Auf dem Wege traf ich meistens Krämer, die nach der Braunschweiger Messe zogen, auch einen Schwarm Frauenzimmer, deren jede ein großes, fast häuserhohes, mit weißem Leinen überzogenes Behältnis auf dem Rükken trug. Darin saßen allerlei eingefangene Singvögel, die beständig piepsten und zwitscherten, während ihre Trägerinnen lustig dahinhüpften und schwatzten. Mir kam es gar närrisch vor, wie so ein Vogel den andern zu Markte trägt.

In pechdunkler Nacht kam ich an zu Osterode. Es fehlte mir der Appetit zum Essen und ich legte mich gleich zu Bette. Ich war müde wie ein Hund und schlief wie ein Gott. Im Traume kam ich wieder nach Göttingen zurück, und zwar nach der dortigen Bibliothek. Ich stand in einer Ecke des juristischen Saals, durchstöberte alte Dissertationen, vertiefte mich im Lesen, und als ich aufhörte, bemerkte ich zu meiner Verwunde-

spectacles cast in turn a verdigris glow upon his copper-red nose. The gentleman's general appearance was that which we may presume King Nebuchadnezzar to have presented after having passed a few years out at grass.[21] The Green One requested me to recommend him to a hotel in Göttingen, and I advised him when there to inquire of the first convenient student for the Hotel de Brübach. One lady was evidently his wife: an altogether extensively constructed dame, gifted with a mile-square countenance, with dimples in her cheeks which looked like hide-and-go-seek holes for well-grown cupids. A copious double chin appeared below, like an imperfect continuation of the face, while her highpiled bosom, which was defended by stiff points of lace, and a many-cornered collar, as if by turrets and bastions, reminded one of a fortress. The other lady, her sister, seemed her extreme antitype. If the one were descended from Pharaoh's fat kine, the other was as certainly derived from the lean.[22] Her face was but a mouth between two ears; her breast was as inconsolably comfortless and dreary as the Lüneburger heath; while her altogether dried-up figure reminded one of a charity table for poor students of theology. Both ladies asked me, in a breath, if respectable people lodged in the Hotel de Brübach? I assented to this question with certainty, and a clear conscience, and as the charming trio drove away, I waved my hand to them many times from the window. The landlord of the "Sun" laughed, however, in his sleeve, being probably aware that the Hotel de Brübach was a name bestowed by the students of Göttingen upon their University prison.

Beyond Nordheim mountain ridges begin to appear, and the traveler occasionally meets with a picturesque eminence. The wayfarers whom I encountered were principally pedlers, traveling to the Brunswick fair, and among them were swarms of women, every one of whom bore on her back an incredibly large pack, covered with linen. In these packs were cages, containing

rung, daß es Nacht war, und herabhängende Kristall-Leuchter den Saal erhellten. Die nahe Kirchenglocke schlug eben zwölf, die Saaltüre öffnete sich langsam, und herein trat eine stolze, gigantische Frau, ehrfurchtsvoll begleitet von den Mitgliedern und Anhängern der juristischen Fakultät. Das Riesenweib, obgleich schon bejahrt, trug dennoch im Antlitz die Züge einer strengen Schönheit, jeder ihrer Blicke verriet die hohe Titanin, die gewaltige Themis. Schwert und Waage hielt sie nachlässig zusammen in der einen Hand, in der andern hielt sie eine Pergamentrolle, zwei junge Doctores juris trugen die Schleppe ihres grau verblichenen Gewandes; an ihrer rechten Seite sprang windig hin und her der dünne Hofrat Rusticus, der Lykurg Hannovers, und deklamierte aus seinem neuen Gesetzentwurf; an ihrer linken Seite humpelte, gar galant und wohlgelaunt, ihr Cavaliere servente, der geheime Justizrat Cujacius, und riß beständig juristische Witze, und lachte selbst darüber so herzlich, daß sogar die ernste Göttin sich mehrmals lächelnd zu ihm herabbeugte, mit der großen Pergamentrolle ihm auf die Schulter klopfte, und freundlich flüsterte:»Kleiner, loser Schalk, der die Bäume von oben herab beschneidet!« Jeder von den übrigen Herren trat jetzt ebenfalls näher und hatte etwas hin zu bemerken und hin zu lächeln, etwa ein neu ergrübeltes Systemchen, oder Hypotheschen, oder ähnliches Mißgebürtchen des eigenen Köpfchens. Durch die geöffnete Saaltüre traten auch noch mehrere fremde Herren herein, die sich als die andern großen Männer des illustren Ordens kund gaben, meistens eckige, lauernde Gesellen, die mit breiter Selbstzufriedenheit gleich drauf los definierten und distinguierten und über jedes Titelchen eines Pandektentitels disputierten. Und immer kamen noch neue Gestalten herein, alte Rechtsgelehrten, in verschollenen Trachten, mit weißen Allongeperucken und längst vergessenen Gesichtern, und sehr erstaunt, daß man sie, die Hochberühmten des verflossenen Jahrhunderts, nicht sonderlich regardierte; und diese stimmten nun ein, auf ihre Weise, in das

every variety of singing birds, which continually chirped and sung, while their bearers merrily hopped along and sang together. A queer fancy came into my head, that I beheld one bird carrying others to market. The night was dark as pitch as I entered Osterode. I had no appetite for supper, and at once went to bed. I was as tired as a dog and slept like a god. In my dreams I returned to Göttingen, even to its very library. I stood in a corner of the Hall of Jurisprudence, turning over old dissertations, lost myself in reading, and when I finally looked up, remarked to my astonishment that it was night, and that the Hall was illuminated by innumerable overhanging crystal chandeliers. The bell of the neighboring church struck twelve, the hall doors slowly opened, and there entered a superb colossal female form, reverentially accompanied by the members and hangers-on of the legal faculty. The giantess though advanced in years retained in her countenance traces of extreme beauty, and her every glance indicated the sublime Titaness, the mighty Themis. The sword and balance were carelessly grasped in her right hand, while with the left she held a roll of parchment. Two young *Doctores Juris* bore the train of her faded gray robe; by her right side the lean Court Counselor Rusticus, the Lycurgus of Hannover,[23] fluttered here and there like a zephyr, declaiming extracts from his last legal essay, while by her left, her cavaliere servants, the privy legal counselor Cajacius,[24] hobbled gaily and gallantly along, constantly cracking legal jokes, laughing himself so heartily at his own wit, that even the serious goddess often smiled and bent over him, exclaiming as she tapped him on the shoulder with the great parchment roll, "Thou little scamp who cuttest down the tree from the top!"[25] All of the gentlemen who formed her escort now drew nigh in turn, each having something to remark or jest over, either a freshly worked up system, or a miserable little hypothesis, or some similar abortion of their own brains.

allgemeine Schwatzen und Schrillen und Schreien, das, wie
Meeresbrandung, immer verwirrter und lauter, die hohe Göttin
umrauschte, bis diese die Geduld verlor, und in einem Tone des
entsetzlichsten Riesenschmerzes plötzlich aufschrie: »Schweigt!
schweigt! ich höre die Stimme des teuren Prometheus, die
höhnende Kraft und die stumme Gewalt schmieden den Schuld-
losen an den Marterfelsen, und all Euer Geschwätz und Gezänke
kann nicht seine Wunden kühlen und seine Fesseln zerbrechen!«
So rief die Göttin, und Tränenbäche stürzten aus ihren Augen,
die ganze Versammlung heulte wie von Todesangst ergriffen,
die Decke des Saales krachte, die Bücher taumelten herab von
ihren Brettern, vergebens trat der alte Münchhausen aus seinem
Rahmen hervor, um Ruhe zu gebieten, es tobte und kreischte
immer wilder, – und fort aus diesem drängenden Tollhauslärm
rettete ich mich in den historischen Saal, nach jener Gnaden-
stelle, wo die heiligen Bilder des belvederischen Apolls und der
mediceischen Venus neben einander stehen, und ich stürzte zu
den Füßen der Schönheitsgöttin, in ihrem Anblick vergaß ich
all das wüste Treiben, dem ich entronnen, meine Augen tranken
entzückt das Ebenmaß und die ewige Lieblichkeit ihres hoch-
gebenedeiten Leibes, griechische Ruhe zog durch meine Seele,
und über mein Haupt, wie himmlischen Segen, goß seine
süßesten Lyraklänge Phöbus Apollo.
    Erwachend hörte ich noch immer ein freundliches Klingen.
Die Herden zogen auf die Weide und es läuteten ihre Glöckchen. Die liebe, goldene Sonne schien durch das Fenster und
beleuchtete die Schildereien an den Wänden des Zimmers. Es
waren Bilder aus dem Befreiungskriege, worauf treu dargestellt
stand, wie wir alle Helden waren, dann auch Hinrichtungs-
Szenen aus der Revolutionszeit, Ludwig XVI. auf der Guillotine, und ähnliche Kopfabschneidereien, die man gar nicht ansehen kann, ohne Gott zu danken, daß man ruhig im Bette liegt,
und guten Kaffee trinkt und den Kopf noch so recht komfor-
tabel auf den Schultern sitzen hat.

Through the open door of the hall now entered many strange gentlemen, who announced themselves as the remaining magnates of the illustrious order; mostly angular suspicious-looking fellows, who with extreme complacency blazed away with their definitions and hair-splittings, disputing over every scrap of a title to the title of a pandect. And other forms continually flocked in, the forms of those who were learned in law in the olden time, men in antiquated costume, with long counselors' wigs and forgotten faces, who expressed themselves greatly astonished that they, the widely famed of the previous century, should not meet with especial consideration; and these, after their manner, joined in the general chattering and screaming, which like ocean breakers became louder and madder around the mighty Goddess, until she, bursting from impatience, suddenly cried, in a tone of the most agonized Titanic pain, "Silence! silence! I hear the voice of the loved Prometheus,[26] mocking cunning and brute force are chaining the innocent One to the rock of martyrdom, and all your prattling and quarreling will not allay his wounds to break his fetters!" So cried the Goddess, and rivulets of tears sprang from her eyes, the entire assembly howled as if in the agonies of death, the ceiling of the hall burst asunder, the books tumbled madly from their shelves, and in vain the portrait of old Münchausen[27] called out "order" from his frame, for all crashed and raged more wildly around. sought refuge from this Bedlam broke loose, in the Hall of History, near that gracious spot where the holy images of the Apollo Belvedere and the Venus de Medici stand near together, and I knelt at the feet of the Goddess of Beauty; in her glance I forgot all the wearisome barren labor which I had passed, my eyes drank in with intoxication the symmetry and immortal loveliness of her infinitely blessed form; Hellenic calm swept through my soul, while above my head, Phoebus Apollo poured forth like heavenly blessings, the sweetest tones of his lyre.

19

Nachdem ich Kaffee getrunken, mich angezogen, die In-
schriften auf den Fensterscheiben gelesen, und alles im Wirtshause berichtigt hatte, verließ ich Osterode.

Diese Stadt hat so und so viel Häuser, verschiedene Ein-
wohner, worunter auch mehrere Seelen, wie in Gottschalks
»Taschenbuch für Harzreisende« genauer nachzulesen ist. Ehe
ich die Landstraße einschlug, bestieg ich die Trümmer der uralten Osteroder Burg. Sie bestehen nur noch aus der Hälfte
eines großen, dickmaurigen, wie von Krebsschäden angefresse-
nen Turms. Der Weg nach Klausthal führte mich wieder bergauf, und von einer der ersten Höhen schaute ich nochmals hinab
in das Tal, wo Osterode mit seinen roten Dächern aus den
grünen Tannenwäldern hervor guckt, wie eine Moosrose. Die
Sonne gab eine gar liebe, kindliche Beleuchtung. Von der er-
haltenen Turmhälfte erblickt man hier die imponierende Rück-
seite.

Nachdem ich eine Strecke gewandert, traf ich zusammen mit
einem reisenden Handwerksburschen, der von Braunschweig
kam und mir als ein dortiges Gerücht erzählte: der junge Herzog
sei auf dem Wege nach dem gelobten Lande von den Türken
gefangen worden, und könne nur gegen ein großes Lösegeld
frei kommen. Die große Reise des Herzogs mag diese Sage ver-
anlaßt haben. Das Volk hat noch immer den traditionell fabel-
haften Ideengang, der sich so lieblich ausspricht in seinem
»Herzog Ernst«. Der Erzähler jener Neuigkeit war ein Schneider-
gesell, ein niedlicher, kleiner junger Mensch, so dünn, daß die
Sterne durchschimmern konnten, wie durch Ossians Nebel-
geister, und im Ganzen eine volkstümlich barocke Mischung
von Laune und Wehmut. Dieses äußerte sich besonders in der
drollig rührenden Weise, womit er das wunderbare Volkslied
sang: »Ein Käfer auf dem Zaune saß; summ, summ!« Das ist
schön bei uns Deutschen; keiner ist so verrückt, daß er nicht
einen noch Verrückteren fände, der ihn versteht. Nur ein
Deutscher kann jenes Lied nachempfinden, und sich dabei tot-

Awaking, I continued to hear a pleasant musical ringing. The flocks were on their way to pasture, and their bells were tinkling. The blessed golden sunlight shone through the window, illuminating the pictures on the walls of my room. They were sketches from the war of Independence,[28] and among them were placed representations of the execution of Louis XVI on the guillotine, and other decapitations which no one could behold without thanking God that he lay quietly in bed, drinking excellent coffee, and with his head comfortably adjusted upon neck and shoulders.

After I had drunk my coffee, dressed myself, read the inscriptions upon the window-panes and set everything straight in the inn, I left Osterode.

This town contains a certain quantity of houses and a given number of inhabitants, among whom are divers and sundry souls, as may be ascertained in detail from Gottschalk's "Pocket Book for Harz Travelers."[29] Ere I struck into the highway I ascended the ruins of the very ancient Osteroder Burg. They consisted of merely the half of a great, thick-walled tower, which appeared to be fairly honey-combed by time. The road to Klausthal led me again uphill, and from one of the first eminences I looked back into the dale where Osterode, with its red roofs, peeps out from among the green fir woods, like a moss-rose from amid its leaves. The pleasant sunlight inspired gentle, childlike feelings. From this spot the imposing rear of the remaining portion of the tower may be seen to advantage.

After proceeding a little distance, I overtook and went along with a traveling craftsman,[30] who came from Brunswick, and related to me that it was generally believed in that city, that their young duke had been taken prisoner by the Turks during his tour in the Holy Land, and could only be ransomed by an enormous sum. The extensive travels of the duke probably originated this tale. The people at large still preserve that traditional fable-loving train of

lachen und totweinen. Wie tief das Goethesche Wort ins Leben des Volks gedrungen, bemerkte ich auch hier. Mein dünner Weggenosse trillerte ebenfalls zuweilen vor sich hin: »Leidvoll und freudvoll, Gedanken sind frei!« Solche Korruption des Textes ist beim Volke etwas Gewöhnliches. Er sang auch ein Lied, wo »Lottchen bei dem Grabe ihres Werthers« trauert. Der Schneider zerfloß vor Sentimentalität bei den Worten: »Einsam wein ich an der Rosenstelle, wo uns oft der späte Mond belauscht! Jammernd irr ich an der Silberquelle, die uns lieblich Wonne zugerauscht.« Aber bald darauf ging er in Mutwillen über, und erzählte mir: »Wir haben einen Preußen in der Herberge zu Kassel, der eben solche Lieder selbst macht; er kann keinen seligen Stich nähen; hat er einen Groschen in der Tasche, so hat er für zwei Groschen Durst, und wenn er im Tran ist, hält er den Himmel für ein blaues Kamisol, und weint wie eine Dachtraufe, und singt ein Lied mit der doppelten Poesie!« Von letzterem Ausdruck wünschte ich eine Erklärung, aber mein Schneiderlein, mit seinen Ziegenhainer Beinchen, hüpfte hin und her und rief beständig: »Die doppelte Poesie ist die doppelte Poesie!« Endlich brachte ich es heraus, daß er doppelt gereimte Gedichte, namentlich Stanzen, im Sinne hatte. – Unterdes, durch die große Bewegung und durch den konträren Wind, war der Ritter von der Nadel sehr müde geworden. Er machte freilich noch einige große Anstalten zum Gehen und bramarbasierte: »Jetzt will ich den Weg zwischen die Beine nehmen!« Doch bald klagte er, daß er sich Blasen unter die Füße gegangen, und die Welt viel zu weitläuftig sei; und endlich, bei einem Baumstamme, ließ er sich sachte niedersinken, bewegte sein zartes Häuptlein wie ein betrübtes Lämmerschwänzchen, und wehmütig lächelnd rief er: »Da bin ich armes Schindluderchen schon wieder marode!«

Die Berge wurden hier noch steiler, die Tannenwälder wogten unten wie ein grünes Meer, und am blauen Himmel oben schifften die weißen Wolken. Die Wildheit der Gegend war

ideas, which is so pleasantly shone in their "Duke Ernst."[31] The narrator of this news was a tailor, a neat little youth, but so thin that the stars might have shone through him as through Ossian's ghosts.[32] Altogether, he formed a vulgar mixture of affectation, whim and melancholy. This was peculiarly expressed in the droll and affecting manner in which he sang that extraordinary popular ballad, "A beetle sat upon the hedge, summ, summ!"[33] That is a pleasant peculiarity of us Germans. No one is so crazy but that he may find a crazier comrade, who will understand him. Only a German can appreciate that song, and in the same breath laugh and cry himself to death over it. On this occasion, I also remarked the depth to which the words of Goethe have penetrated into the national life. My lean comrade trilled occasionally as he went along. "Joyful and sorrowful, thoughts are free!" Such a corruption of a text is usual among the multitude.[34] He also sang a song in which Lottie by the grave of Werther wept.[35] The tailor ran over with sentimentalism in the words, "Sadly by the rose beds now I weep, where the late moon found us oft alone! Moaning where the silver fountains sleep, which rippled once delight in every tone." But he soon became capricious and petulant remarking, that "We have a Prussian in the tavern at Cassel, who makes exactly such songs, himself. He can't sew a single decent stitch; when he has a penny in his pocket he always has twopence worth of thirst with it, and when he has a drop in his eye, he takes heaven to be a blue jacket, weeps like a roof spout, and sings a song with double poetry." I desired an explanation of this last expression, but my tailoring friend hopped about on his walking-cane legs and cried incessantly, "Double poetry is double poetry, and nothing else." Finally, I ascertained that he meant doubly rhymed poems, or stanzas. Meanwhile, owing to his extra exertion, and an adverse wind, the knight of the needle became sadly weary. It is true that he still made a great pretense of advancing, and blustered, "Now I will take the road between my

23

durch ihre Einheit und Einfachheit gleichsam gezähmt. Wie ein guter Dichter, liebt die Natur keine schroffen Übergänge. Die Wolken, so bizarr gestaltet sie auch zuweilen erscheinen, tragen ein weißes, oder doch ein mildes, mit dem blauen Himmel und der grünen Erde harmonisch korrespondierendes Kolorit, so daß alle Farben einer Gegend wie leise Musik in einander schmelzen, und jeder Naturanblick krampfstillend und gemütberuhigend wirkt. – Der selige Hoffmann würde die Wolken buntscheckig bemalt haben. – Eben wie ein großer Dichter, weiß die Natur auch mit den wenigsten Mitteln die größten Effekte hervorzubringen. Da sind nur eine Sonne, Bäume, Blumen, Wasser und Liebe. Freilich, fehlt letztere im Herzen des Beschauers, so mag das Ganze wohl einen schlechten Anblick gewähren, und die Sonne hat dann bloß so und so viel Meilen im Durchmesser, und die Bäume sind gut zum Einheizen, und die Blumen werden nach den Staubfäden klassifiziert, und das Wasser ist naß.

Ein kleiner Junge, der für seinen kranken Oheim im Walde Reisig suchte, zeigte mir das Dorf Lerbach, dessen kleine Hütten, mit grauen Dächern, sich über eine halbe Stunde durch das Tal hinziehen.»Dort«, sagte er, »wohnen dumme Kropfleute und weiße Mohren«, – mit letzterem Namen werden die Albinos vom Volke benannt. Der kleine Junge stand mit den Bäumen in gar eigenem Einverständnis; er grüßte sie wie gute Bekannte, und sie schienen rauschend seinen Gruß zu erwidern. Er pfiff wie ein Zeisig, ringsum antworteten zwitschernd die andern Vögel, und ehe ich mich dessen versah, war er mit seinen nackten Füßchen und seinem Bündel Reisig ins Walddickicht fortgesprungen. Die Kinder, dacht ich, sind jünger als wir, können sich noch erinnern, wie sie ebenfalls Bäume oder Vögel waren, und sind also noch im Stande, dieselben zu verstehen; unsereins aber ist schon alt und hat zu viel Sorgen, Jurisprudenz und schlechte Verse im Kopf. Jene Zeit, wo es anders war, trat mir bei meinem Eintritt in Klausthal wieder recht lebhaft ins Ge-

legs." But he, immediately after, explained that his feet were blistered, and that the world was by far too extensive, and finally sinking down at the foot of a tree, he moved his delicate little head like the tail of a troubled lamb, and wofully smiling, murmured, "Here am I, poor vagabond, already again weary!"

The hills here became steeper, the fir woods waved below like a green sea, and white clouds above sailed along over the blue sky. The wildness of the region was, however, tamed by its uniformity and the simplicity of its elements. Nature, like a true poet, abhors abrupt transitions. Clouds—however fantastically formed they may at times appear—still have a white, or at least a subdued, hue, harmoniously corresponding with the blue heaven and the green earth; so that all the colors of a landscape blend into each other like soft music, every glance at such a natural picture tranquilizes and reassures the soul. The late Hoffman would have painted the clouds spotted and checkered.[36] And like a great poet, Nature knows how to produce the greatest effects with the most limited means. There she has only a sun, trees and flowers, water and love. Of course, if the latter be lacking in the heart of the observer, the whole will, in all probability, present but a poor appearance, the sun will be so and so many miles in diameter, the trees are for firewood, the flowers are classified according to their stamens, and the water is wet.

A little boy who was gathering brushwood in the forest for his sick uncle, pointed out to me the village of Lerrbach, whose little huts with gray roofs scatter along for two miles through the valley. "There," said he, "live idiots with goiters, and white negroes."[37] By white negroes the people mean albinos. The little fellow lived on terms of peculiar understanding with the trees, addressing them like old acquaintances, while they in turn seemed by their waving and rustling to return his salutations. He chirped like a thistlefinch, many birds around answered his call, and, ere I was aware, he had

dächtnis. In dieses nette Bergstädtchen, welches man nicht früher erblickt, als bis man davor steht, gelangte ich, als eben die Glocke zwölf schlug und die Kinder jubelnd aus der Schule kamen. Die lieben Knaben, fast alle rotbäckig, blauäugig und flachshaarig, sprangen und jauchzten, und weckten in mir die wehmütig heitere Erinnerung, wie ich einst selbst, als ein kleines Bübchen, in einer dumpf-katholischen Klosterschule zu Düsseldorf den ganzen lieben Vormittag von der hölzernen Bank nicht aufstehen durfte, und so viel Latein, Prügel und Geographie ausstehen mußte, und dann ebenfalls unmäßig jauchzte und jubelte, wenn die alte Franziskanerglocke endlich zwölf schlug. Die Kinder sahen an meinem Ranzen, daß ich ein Fremder sei, und grüßten mich recht gastfreundlich. Einer der Knaben erzählte mir, sie hätten eben Religionsunterricht gehabt, und er zeigte mir den Königl. Hannöv. Katechismus, nach welchem man ihnen das Christentum abfragt. Dieses Büchlein war sehr schlecht gedruckt, und ich fürchte, die Glaubenslehren machen dadurch schon gleich einen unerfreulich löschpapierigen Eindruck auf die Gemüter der Kinder; wie es mir denn auch erschrecklich mißfiel, daß das Einmaleins, welches doch mit der heiligen Dreiheitslehre bedenklich kollidiert, im Katechismus selbst, und zwar auf dem letzten Blatte desselben, abgedruckt ist, und die Kinder dadurch schon frühzeitig zu sündhaften Zweifeln verleitet werden können. Da sind wir im Preußischen viel klüger, und bei unserem Eifer zur Bekehrung jener Leute, die sich so gut aufs Rechnen verstehen, hüten wir uns wohl, das Einmaleins hinter dem Katechismus abdrucken zu lassen.

In der »Krone« zu Klausthal hielt ich Mittag. Ich bekam frühlingsgrüne Petersiliensuppe, veilchenblauen Kohl, einen Kalbsbraten, groß wie der Chimborasso in Miniatur, so wie auch eine Art geräucherter Heringe, die Bückinge heißen, nach dem Namen ihres Erfinders, Wilhelm Bücking, der 1447 gestorben, und um jener Erfindung willen von Karl V. so verehrt wurde, daß derselbe anno 1556 von Middelburg nach Bievlied

disappeared with his little bare feet and his bundle of brush, amid the thickets. "Children," thought I, "are younger than we, they can perhaps remember when they were once trees or birds, and are, consequently, still able to understand them. We of larger growth are, alas, too old for that, and carry about in our heads too much legal lore, and too many sorrows and bad verses." But the time when it was otherwise, recurred vividly to me as I entered Klausthal. In this pretty little mountain town, which the traveler does not behold until he stands directly before it, I arrived just as the clock was striking twelve and the children came tumbling merrily out of school. The little rogues, nearly all red-cheecked, blue-eyed, flaxen-haired, sprang and shouted and awoke in me melancholy and cheerful memories, how I once myself, as a little boy, sat all the forenoon long in a gloomy Catholic cloister school in Düsseldorf, without so much as daring to stand up, enduring meanwhile such a terrible amount of Latin, whipping and geography, and how I, too, hurrahed and rejoiced beyond all measure when the old Franciscan clock at last struck twelve. The children saw by my knapsack that I was a stranger, and greeted me in the most hospitable manner. One of the boys told me that they had just had a lesson in religion, and showed me the *Royal Hannoverian Catechism,* from which they were questioned on Christianity. This little book was very badly printed, so that I greatly feared that the doctrines of faith made thereby but an unpleasant blotting-paper sort of impression upon the children's minds. I was also shocked at observing that the multiplication table contrasted with the Holy Trinity on the last page of the catechism, as it at once occurred to me that by this means the minds of the children might, even in their earliest years, be led to the most sinful skepticism. We Prussians are more intelligent, and in our zeal for converting those heathens who are familiar with arithmetic, take good care not to print the multiplication table behind the catechism.[38]

in Seeland reiste, bloß um dort das Grab dieses großen Mannes zu sehen. Wie herrlich schmeckt doch solch ein Gericht, wenn man die historischen Notizen dazu weiß und es selbst verzehrt! Nur der Kaffee nach Tische wurde mir verleidet, indem sich ein junger Mensch diskursierend zu mir setzte und so entsetzlich schwadronierte, daß die Milch auf dem Tische sauer wurde. Es war ein junger Handlungsbeflissener mit fünfundzwanzig bunten Westen und eben so viel goldenen Petschaften, Ringen, Brustnadeln usw. Er sah aus wie ein Affe, der eine rote Jacke angezogen hat und nun zu sich selber sagt: Kleider machen Leute. Eine ganze Menge Charaden wußte er auswendig, so wie auch Anekdoten, die er immer da anbrachte, wo sie am wenigsten paßten. Er fragte mich, was es in Göttingen Neues gäbe, und ich erzählte ihm: daß vor meiner Abreise von dort ein Dekret des akademischen Senats erschienen, worin bei drei Taler Strafe verboten wird, den Hunden die Schwänze abzuschneiden, indem die tollen Hunde in den Hundstagen die Schwänze zwischen den Beinen tragen, und man sie dadurch von den Nichttollen unterscheidet, was doch nicht geschehen könnte, wenn sie gar keine Schwänze haben. – Nach Tische machte ich mich auf den Weg, die Gruben, die Silberhütten und die Münze zu besuchen.

In den Silberhütten habe ich, wie oft im Leben, den Silberblick verfehlt. In der Münze traf ich es schon besser, und konnte zusehen, wie das Geld gemacht wird. Freilich, weiter hab ich es auch nie bringen können. Ich hatte bei solcher Gelegenheit immer das Zusehen, und ich glaube, wenn mal die Taler vom Himmel herunter regneten, so bekäme ich davon nur Löcher in den Kopf, während die Kinder Israel die silberne Manna mit lustigem Mute einsammeln würden. Mit einem Gefühle, worin gar komisch Ehrfurcht und Rührung gemischt waren, betrachtete ich die neugebornen, blanken Taler, nahm einen, der eben vom Prägstocke kam, in die Hand, und sprach zu ihm: junger Taler! welche Schicksale erwarten dich! wie viel Gutes und wie viel

I dined in the "Crown," at Klausthal. My repast consisted of spring green, parsley soup, violet-blue cabbage, a pile of roast veal which resembled Chimborazo in miniature,[39] and a sort of smoked herrings, called "Bückings," from their inventor, William Bücking,[40] who died in 1447, and who on account of the invention was so greatly honored by Charles V that the great monarch in 1556 made a journey from Middleburg to Bievlied in Zealand, for the express purpose of visiting the grave of the great fish drier. How exquisitely such dishes taste when we are familiar with their historical associations! Unfortunately, my after-dinner coffee was spoiled by a youth, who in conversing with me ran on in such an outrageous strain of noise and vanity that the milk was soured. He was a young counter jumper, wearing twenty-five variegated waistcoats, and as many gold seals, rings, breastpins, etc. He seemed like a monkey who having put on a red coat had resolved within himself that clothes make the man. This gentleman had got by heart a vast amount of charades and anecdotes, which he continually repeated in the most inappropriate places. He asked for the news in Göttingen, and I informed him that a decree had been recently published there by the Academical Senate, forbidding any one, under penalty of three dollars, to dock puppies' tails—because during the dog-days, mad dogs invariably ran with their tails between their legs, thus giving a warning indication of the existence of hydrophobia, which could not be perceived were the caudal appendage absent. After dinner I went forth to visit the mines, the mint, and the silver refineries.

In the silver refinery, as has frequently been my luck in life, I could get no glimpse of the precious metal. In the mint I succeeded better, and saw how money was made. Beyond this I have never been able to advance. On such occasions, mine has invariably been the spectator's part, and I verily believe, that if it should rain dollars from Heaven, the coins would only knock holes in my head,

Böses wirst du stiften! wie wirst du das Laster beschützen und
die Tugend flicken, wie wirst du geliebt und dann wieder verwünscht werden! wie wirst du schwelgen, kuppeln, lügen und
morden helfen! wie wirst du rastlos umherirren, durch reine
und schmutzige Hände, jahrhundertelang, bis du endlich,
schuldbeladen und sündenmüd, versammelt wirst zu den Deinen
im Schoße Abrahams, der dich einschmelzt und läutert und
umbildet zu einem neuen besseren Sein.

Das Befahren der zwei vorzüglichsten Klausthaler Gruben,
der »Dorothea« und »Carolina«, fand ich sehr interessant und ich
muß ausführlich davon erzählen.

Eine halbe Stunde vor der Stadt gelangt man zu zwei großen
schwärzlichen Gebäuden. Dort wird man gleich von den Berg-
leuten in Empfang genommen. Diese tragen dunkle, gewöhnlich stahlblaue, weite, bis über den Bauch herabhängende
Jacken, Hosen von ähnlicher Farbe, ein hinten aufgebundenes
Schurzfell und kleine grüne Filzhüte, ganz randlos, wie ein ab-
gekappter Kegel. In eine solche Tracht, bloß ohne Hinterleder,
wird der Besuchende ebenfalls eingekleidet, und ein Bergmann,
ein Steiger, nachdem er sein Grubenlicht angezündet, führt ihn
nach einer dunklen Öffnung, die wie ein Kaminfegeloch aus-
sieht, steigt bis an die Brust hinab, gibt Regeln, wie man sich
an den Leitern fest zu halten habe, und bittet angstlos zu folgen.
Die Sache selbst ist nichts weniger als gefährlich; aber man
glaubt es nicht im Anfang, wenn man gar nichts vom Berg-
werkswesen versteht. Es gibt schon eine eigene Empfindung,
daß man sich ausziehen und die dunkle Delinquententracht an-
ziehen muß. Und nun soll man auf allen Vieren hinab klettern,
und das dunkle Loch ist so dunkel, und Gott weiß, wie lang die
Leiter sein mag. Aber bald merkt man doch, daß es nicht eine
einzige, in die schwarze Ewigkeit hinablaufende Leiter ist,
sondern daß es mehrere von funfzehn bis zwanzig Sprossen
sind, deren jede auf ein kleines Brett leitet, worauf man stehen
kann, und worin wieder ein neues Loch nach einer neuen

while the children of Israel would merrily gather up the silver manna. With feelings in which comic reverence was blended with emotion, I beheld the new-born shining dollars, took one as it came fresh from the stamp, in my hand, and said to it: "Young Dollar! what a destiny awaits thee! what a cause wilt thou be of good and of evil! How thou wilt protect vice and patch up virtue, how thou wilt be beloved and accursed! how thou wilt aid in debauchery, pandering, lying, and murdering! how thou wilt restlessly roll along through clean and dirty hands for centuries, until finally laden with trespasses, and weary with sin, thou wilt be gathered again unto thine own, in the bosom of an Abraham, who will melt thee down and purify thee, and form thee into a new and better being!"

I will narrate in detail my visit to Dorothea and Caroline, the two principal Klausthaler mines, having found them very interesting.

Half a German mile from the town are situated two large, dingy buildings. Here the traveler is transferred to the care of the miners. These men wear dark, and generally steel-blue colored, jackets, of ample girth, descending to the hips, with pantaloons of a similar hue, a leather apron bound on behind, and a rimless green felt hat, which resembles a decapitated ninepin.[41] In such a garb, with the exception of the back leather, the visitor is also clad, and a miner, his leader, after lighting his mine lamp, conducts him to a gloomy entrance, resembling a chimney hole, descends as far as the breast, gives him a few directions relative to grasping the ladder, and carelessly requests him to follow. The affair is entirely devoid of danger, though it at first appears quite otherwise to those unacquainted with the mysteries of mining. Even the putting on of the dark convict dress awakens very peculiar sensations. Then one must clamber down on all fours, the dark hole is so very dark, and Lord only knows how long the ladder

Leiter hinabführt. Ich war zuerst in die Carolina gestiegen. Das ist die schmutzigste und unerfreulichste Carolina, die ich je kennen gelernt habe. Die Leitersprossen sind kotig naß. Und von einer Leiter zur andern gehts hinab, und der Steiger voran, und dieser beteuert immer: es sei gar nicht gefährlich, nur müsse man sich mit den Händen fest an den Sprossen halten, und nicht nach den Füßen sehen, und nicht schwindlicht werden, und nur bei Leibe nicht auf das Seitenbrett treten, wo jetzt das schnurrende Tonnenseil heraufgeht, und wo, vor vierzehn Tagen, ein unvorsichtiger Mensch hinunter gestürzt und leider den Hals gebrochen. Da unten ist ein verworrenes Rauschen und Summen, man stößt beständig an Balken und Seile, die in Bewegung sind, um die Tonnen mit geklopften Erzen, oder das hervorgesinterte Wasser, herauf zu winden. Zuweilen gelangt man auch in durchgehauene Gänge, Stollen genannt, wo man das Erz wachsen sieht, und wo der einsame Bergmann den ganzen Tag sitzt und mühsam mit dem Hammer die Erzstücke aus der Wand heraus klopft. Bis in die unterste Tiefe, wo man, wie einige behaupten, schon hören kann, wie die Leute in Amerika »Hurrah Lafayette!« schreien, bin ich nicht gekommen; unter uns gesagt, dort, bis wohin ich kam, schien es mir bereits tief genug: – immerwährendes Brausen und Sausen, unheimliche Maschinenbewegung, unterirdisches Quellengeriesel, von allen Seiten herabtriefendes Wasser, qualmig aufsteigende Erddünste, und das Grubenlicht immer bleicher hinein flimmernd in die einsame Nacht. Wirklich, es war betäubend, das Atmen wurde mir schwer, und mit Mühe hielt ich mich an den glitschrigen Leitersprossen. Ich habe keinen Anflug von sogenannter Angst empfunden, aber, seltsam genug, dort unten in der Tiefe erinnerte ich mich, daß ich im vorigen Jahre, ungefähr um dieselbe Zeit, einen Sturm auf der Nordsee erlebte, und ich meinte jetzt, es sei doch eigentlich recht traulich angenehm, wenn das Schiff hin und her schaukelt, die Winde ihre Trompeterstückchen losblasen, zwischendrein der lustige Matrosen-

may be! But we soon remark that this is not the only ladder in the black eternity around, for there are many of from fifteen to twenty rounds apiece, each standing upon a board capable of supporting a man, and from which a new hole leads in turn to a new ladder. I first entered the Caroline, the dirtiest and most disagreeable of that name with whom I ever had the pleasure of becoming acquainted. The rounds of the ladders were covered with wet mud. And from one ladder we descended to another, with the guide ever in advance, continually assuring us that there is no danger so long as we hold firmly to the rounds and do not look at our feet, and that we must not for our lives tread on the side plank, where the buzzing barrel rope runs, and where two weeks ago a careless man was knocked down, unfortunately breaking his neck by the fall. Far below is a confused rustling and humming, and we continually bump against beams and ropes which are in motion, winding up and raising barrels of broken ore or of water. Occasionally we pass galleries hewn in the rock, called "stulms," where the ore may be seen growing, and where some solitary miner sits the livelong day, wearily hammering pieces from the walls. I did not descend to those deepest depths, where it is reported that the people on the other side of the world, in America, may be heard crying, "Hurrah for Lafayette!"[42] Where I went seemed to me, however, deep enough in all conscience; amid an endless roaring and rattling, the mysterious sounds of machinery, the rush of subterranean streams, the sickening clouds of ore dust continually rising, water dripping on all the sides, and the miner's lamp gradually growing dimmer and dimmer. The effect was really benumbing, I breathed with difficulty, and held with trouble to the slippery rounds. It was not fright which overpowered me, but oddly enough, down there in the depths, I remembered that a year before, about the same time, I had been in a storm on the North Sea,[43] and I now felt

lärmen erschallt und alles frisch überschauert wird von Gottes lieber, freier Luft. Ja, Luft! – Nach Luft schnappend stieg ich einige Dutzend Leitern wieder in die Höhe, und mein Steiger führte mich durch einen schmalen, sehr langen, in den Berg gehauenen Gang nach der Grube Dorothea. Hier ist es luftiger und frischer, und die Leitern sind reiner, aber auch länger und steiler als in der Carolina. Hier wurde mir schon besser zu Mute, besonders da ich wieder Spuren lebendiger Menschen gewahrte. In der Tiefe zeigten sich nämlich wandelnde Schimmer; Bergleute mit ihren Grubenlichtern kamen allmählig in die Höhe, mit dem Gruße »Glückauf!« und mit demselben Wiedergruße von unserer Seite stiegen sie an uns vorüber; und wie eine befreundet ruhige, und doch zugleich quälend rätselhafte Erinnerung, trafen mich, mit ihren tiefsinnig klaren Blicken, die ernstfrommen, etwas blassen, und vom Grubenlicht geheimnisvoll beleuchteten Gesichter dieser jungen und alten Männer, die in ihren dunkeln, einsamen Bergschachten den ganzen Tag gearbeitet hatten, und sich jetzt hinauf sehnten nach dem lieben Tageslicht, und nach den Augen von Weib und Kind.

Mein Cicerone selbst war eine kreuzehrliche, pudeldeutsche Natur. Mit innerer Freudigkeit zeigte er mir jene Stolle, wo der Herzog von Cambridge, als er die Grube befahren, mit seinem ganzen Gefolge gespeist hat, und wo noch der lange hölzerne Speisetisch steht, so wie auch der große Stuhl von Erz, worauf der Herzog gesessen. Dieser bleibe zum ewigen Andenken stehen, sagte der gute Bergmann, und mit Feuer erzählte er: wie viele Festlichkeiten damals statt gefunden, wie der ganze Stollen mit Lichtern, Blumen und Laubwerk verziert gewesen, wie ein Bergknappe die Zither gespielt und gesungen, wie der vergnügte, liebe, dicke Herzog sehr viele Gesundheiten ausgetrunken habe, und wie viele Bergleute, und er selbst ganz besonders, sich gern würden tot schlagen lassen für den lieben, dicken Herzog und das ganze Haus Hannover. – Innig rührt es

that it would be an agreeable change could I feel the rocking of the ship, hear the wind with its thunder-trumpet tones, while amid its lulls sounded the hearty cry of the sailors, and all above was freshly swept by God's own free air. Yes, Air!—Panting for air, I rapidly climbed several dozens of ladders, and my guide led me through a narrow and very long gallery toward the Dorothea mine. Here it is airier and fresher, and the ladders are cleaner, though at the same time longer than in the Caroline. I felt revived and more cheerful, particularly as I observed indications of human beings. Far below I saw wandering, wavering lights, miners with their lamps came one by one upwards with the greeting, "Good luck to you!" and receiving the same salutation from us, went onwards and upwards. Something like a friendly and quiet, yet at the same time terrific and enigmatical, recollection flitted across my mind as I met the deep glances and earnest, pale faces of these men, mysteriously illuminated by their lanterns, and thought how they had worked all day in lonely and secret places in the mines, and how they now longed for the blessed light of day, and for the glances of wives and children.

My guide himself was a thoroughly honest, honorable, blundering German being. With inward joy he pointed out to me the stulm where the Duke of Cambridge,[44] when he visited the mines, dined with all his train, and where the long wooden table yet stands, with the accompanying great chair, made of ore, in which the Duke sat. "This is to remain as an eternal memorial," said the good miner, and he related with enthusiasm how many festivities had then taken place, how the entire stulm had been adorned with lamps, flowers, and decorations of leaves; how a miner boy had played on the cither and sung; how the dear, delighted fat Duke had drained many healths, and what a number of miners (himself especially) would cheerfully die for the dear, fat Duke, and for the whole house of Hannover. I am moved to my very

mich jedesmal, wenn ich sehe, wie sich dieses Gefühl der Unter-
tanstreue in seinen einfachen Naturlauten ausspricht. Es ist ein
so schönes Gefühl! Und es ist ein so wahrhaft deutsches Gefühl! Andere Völker mögen gewandter sein, und witziger und
ergötzlicher, aber keines ist so treu, wie das treue deutsche
Volk. Wüßte ich nicht, daß die Treue so alt ist, wie die Welt,
so würde ich glauben, ein deutsches Herz habe sie erfunden.
Deutsche Treue! sie ist keine moderne Adressenfloskel. An
Euren Höfen, Ihr deutschen Fürsten, sollte man singen und
wieder singen das Lied von dem getreuen Eckart und dem
bösen Burgund, der ihm die lieben Kinder töten lassen, und ihn
alsdann doch noch immer treu befunden hat. Ihr habt das
treueste Volk, und Ihr irrt, wenn Ihr glaubt, der alte, ver-
ständige, treue Hund sei plötzlich toll geworden, und schnappe
nach Euren geheiligten Waden.

Wie die deutsche Treue, hatte uns jetzt das kleine Grubenlicht, ohne viel Geflacker, still und sicher geleitet durch das
Labyrinth der Schachten und Stollen; wir stiegen hervor aus
der dumpfigen Bergnacht, das Sonnenlicht strahlt' – Glück
auf!

Die meisten Bergarbeiter wohnen in Klausthal und in dem
damit verbundenen Bergstädtchen Zellerfeld. Ich besuchte
mehrere dieser wackern Leute, betrachtete ihre kleine häusliche
Einrichtung, hörte einige ihrer Lieder, die sie mit der Zither,
ihrem Lieblingsinstrumente, gar hübsch begleiten, ließ mir alte
Bergmärchen von ihnen erzählen, und auch die Gebete her-
sagen, die sie in Gemeinschaft zu halten pflegen, ehe sie in den
dunkeln Schacht hinunter steigen, und manches gute Gebet
habe ich mit gebetet. Ein alter Steiger meinte sogar, ich sollte
bei ihnen bleiben und Bergmann werden; und als ich dennoch
Abschied nahm, gab er mir einen Auftrag an seinen Bruder,
der in der Nähe von Goslar wohnt, und viele Küsse für seine
liebe Nichte.

So stillstehend ruhig auch das Leben dieser Leute erscheint,

heart when I see loyalty thus manifested in all its natural simplicity. It is such a beautiful sentiment! And such a purely German sentiment! Other people may be more intelligent and wittier, and more agreeable, but none are so faithful as the real German race. Did I not know that fidelity is as old as the world, I would believe that a German had invented it. German fidelity is no modern "yours very truly," or, "I remain your humble servant." In your courts, ye German princes, ye should cause to be sung, and sung again, the old ballad of "The trusty Eckhart and the base Burgund,"[45] who slew Eckhart's seven children, and still found him faithful. Ye have the truest people in the world, and ye err when ye deem that the old, intelligent, trusty hound has suddenly gone mad, and snaps at your sacred calves!

And like German fidelity, the little mine lamp has guided us quietly and securely, without much flickering or flaring, through the labyrinths of shafts and stulms. We jump from the gloomy mountain night—sunlight flashes around, "Luck to you"!

Most of the miners dwell in Klausthal, and in the adjoining small town of Zellerfeld. I visited several of these brave fellows, observed their little household arrangements, heard many of their songs, which they skilfully accompany with their favorite instrument, the cither, and listened to old mining legends, and to their prayers, which they are accustomed to offer daily in company ere they descend the gloomy shaft. And many a good prayer did I offer up with them. One old climber even thought that I ought to remain among them, and become a man of the mines, and as I, after all, departed, he gave me a message to his brother, who dwelt near Goslar, and many kisses for his darling niece.

Immovably tranquil as the life of these men may appear, it is, notwithstanding, a real and vivid life. That ancient, trembling crone who sits before the great clothes-press and behind the

so ist es dennoch ein wahrhaftes, lebendiges Leben. Die stein-
alte, zitternde Frau, die, dem großen Schranke gegenüber,
hinterm Ofen saß, mag dort schon ein Vierteljahrhundert lang
gesessen haben, und ihr Denken und Fühlen ist gewiß innig
verwachsen mit allen Ecken dieses Ofens und allen Schnitzeleien
dieses Schrankes. Und Schrank und Ofen leben, denn ein
Mensch hat ihnen einen Teil seiner Seele eingeflößt.

Nur durch solch tiefes Anschauungsleben, durch die »Un-
mittelbarkeit« entstand die deutsche Märchenfabel, deren
Eigentümlichkeit darin besteht, daß nicht nur die Tiere und
Pflanzen, sondern auch ganz leblos scheinende Gegenstände
sprechen und handeln. Sinnigem, harmlosen Volke, in der
stillen, umfriedeten Heimlichkeit seiner niedern Berg- oder
Waldhütten offenbarte sich das innere Leben solcher Gegenstände, diese gewannen einen notwendigen, konsequenten
Charakter, eine süße Mischung von phantastischer Laune und
rein menschlicher Gesinnung; und so sehen wir im Märchen,
wunderbar und doch als wenn es sich von selbst verstände:
Nähnadel und Stecknadel kommen von der Schneiderherberge
und verirren sich im Dunkeln; Strohhalm und Kohle wollen
über den Bach setzen und verunglücken; Schippe und Besen
stehen auf der Treppe und zanken und schmeißen sich; der
befragte Spiegel zeigt das Bild der schönsten Frau; sogar die
Blutstropfen fangen an zu sprechen, bange, dunkle Worte des
besorglichsten Mitleids. – Aus demselben Grunde ist unser
Leben in der Kindheit so unendlich bedeutend, in jener Zeit ist
uns alles gleich wichtig, wir hören alles, wir sehen alles, bei
allen Eindrücken ist Gleichmäßigkeit, statt daß wir späterhin
absichtlicher werden, uns mit dem Einzelnen ausschließlicher
beschäftigen, das klare Gold der Anschauung für das Papiergeld
der Bücherdefinitionen mühsam einwechseln, und an Lebens-
breite gewinnen, was wir an Lebenstiefe verlieren. Jetzt sind
wir ausgewachsene, vornehme Leute; wir beziehen oft neue
Wohnungen, die Magd räumt täglich auf, und verändert nach

stove, may have been there for a quarter of a century, and all her thinking and feeling is, beyond a doubt, intimately blended with every corner of the stove and the carvings of the press. And the clothes-press and stove live, for a human being hath breathed into them a portion of its soul.

Only a life of this deep looking into phenomena and its "immediateness "could originate the German popular tale whose peculiarity consists in this, that in it, not only animals and plants, but also objects apparently inanimate, speak and act. To thinking, harmless beings who dwelt in the quiet homeness of their lowly mountain cabins or forest huts, the inner life of these objects was gradually revealed, they acquired a necessary and consequential character, a sweet blending of fantasy and pure human reflection. This is the reason why, in such fables, we find the extreme of singularity allied to a spirit of perfect self-intelligence, as when the pin and the needle wander forth from the tailor's home and are bewildered in the dark; when the straw and the coal seek to cross the brook and are destroyed; when the dust-pan and broom quarrel and fight on the stairs; when the interrogated mirror of Snowdrop shows the image of the fairest lady, and when even drops of blood begin to utter dark words of the deepest compassion.[46] And this is the reason why our life in childhood is so infinitely significant, for then all things are of the same importance, nothing escapes our attention, there is equality in every impression; while, when more advanced in years, we must act with design, busy ourselves more exclusively with particulars, carefully exchange the pure gold of observation for the paper currency of book definitions, and win in the breadth of life what we have lost in depth. Now, we are grown-up, respectable people, we often inhabit new dwellings, the housemaid daily cleans them, and changes at her will the position of the furniture which interests us but little, as it is either new, or may belong

Gutdünken die Stellung der Möbeln, die uns wenig interessieren, da sie entweder neu sind, oder heute dem Hans, morgen dem Isaak gehören; selbst unsere Kleider bleiben uns fremd, wir wissen kaum, wie viel Knöpfe an dem Rocke sitzen, den wir eben jetzt auf dem Leibe tragen; wir wechseln ja so oft als möglich mit Kleidungsstücken, keines derselben bleibt im Zusammenhange mit unserer inneren und äußeren Geschichte; – kaum vermögen wir uns zu erinnern, wie jene braune Weste aussah, die uns einst so viel Gelächter zugezogen hat, und auf deren breiten Streifen dennoch die liebe Hand der Geliebten so lieblich ruhte!

Die alte Frau, dem großen Schrank gegenüber, hinterm Ofen, trug einen geblümten Rock von verschollenem Zeuge, das Brautkleid ihrer seligen Mutter. Ihr Urenkel, ein als Bergmann gekleideter, blonder, blitzäugiger Knabe, saß zu ihren Füßen und zählte die Blumen ihres Rockes, und sie mag ihm von diesem Rocke wohl schon viele Geschichtchen erzählt haben, viele ernsthafte, hübsche Geschichten, die der Junge gewiß nicht so bald vergißt, die ihm noch oft vorschweben werden, wenn er bald, als ein erwachsener Mann, in den nächtlichen Stollen der Carolina einsam arbeitet, und die er vielleicht wieder erzählt, wenn die liebe Großmutter längst tot ist, und er selber, ein silberhaariger, erloschener Greis, im Kreise seiner Enkel sitzt, dem großen Schranke gegenüber, hinterm Ofen.

Ich blieb die Nacht ebenfalls in der »Krone«, wo unterdessen auch der Hofrat B. aus Göttingen angekommen war. Ich hatte das Vergnügen, dem alten Herrn meine Aufwartung zu machen. Als ich mich ins Fremdenbuch einschrieb und im Monat Juli blätterte, fand ich auch den vielteuern Namen Adalbert von Chamisso, den Biographen des unsterblichen Schlemihl. Der Wirt erzählte mir: dieser Herr sei in einem unbeschreibbar schlechten Wetter angekommen, und in einem eben so schlechten Wetter wieder abgereist.

Den andern Morgen mußte ich meinen Ranzen nochmals

to-day to Jack, tomorrow to Isaac. Even our very clothes are strange to us, we hardly know how many buttons there are on the coat we wear—for we change our garments as often as possible, and none of them remain deeply identified with our external or inner history. We scarce dare to think how that brown vest once looked, which attracted so much laughter, and yet on the broad stripes of which the dear hand of the loved one so gently rested!

The old dame who sat before the clothes-press and behind the stove, wore a flowered dress of some old-fashioned material, which had been the bridal robe of her long-buried mother. Her great-grandson, a flashing-eyed blond boy, clad in a miner's dress, knelt at her feet, and counted the flowers on her dress. It may be that she has narrated to him many a story connected with that dress: serious or pretty stories which the boy will not readily forget, which will often recur to him when he, a grown-up man, works alone in the midnight galleries of the Caroline, and which he in turn will narrate when the dear grandmother has long been dead; and he himself, a silver-haired, tranquil old man, sits amid the circle of his grandchildren before the great clothes-press and behind the oven.

I lodged that night in the "Crown," where I had the pleasure of meeting and paying my respects to the old Court Counselor B. of Göttingen.[47] Having inscribed my name in the book of arrivals, I found therein the honored autograph of Adalbert von Chamisso, the biographer of the immortal "Schlemihl." The landlord remarked of Chamisso,[48] that the gentleman had arrived during one terrible storm, and departed in another.

Finding the next morning that I must lighten my knapsack, I threw overboard the pair of boots, and arose and went forth unto Goslar. There I arrived without knowing how. This much alone do I remember, that I sauntered up and down hill, gazing

erleichtern, das eingepackte Paar Stiefel warf ich über Bord, und ich hob auf meine Füße und ging nach Goslar. Ich kam dahin, ohne zu wissen wie. Nur so viel kann ich mich erinnern: ich schlenderte wieder bergauf, bergab; schaute hinunter in manches hübsche Wiesental; silberne Wasser brausten, süße Waldvögel zwitscherten, die Herdenglöckchen läuteten, die mannigfaltig grünen Bäume wurden von der lieben Sonne goldig angestrahlt, und oben war die blauseidene Decke des Himmels so durchsichtig, daß man tief hinein schauen konnte, bis ins Allerheiligste, wo die Engel zu den Füßen Gottes sitzen, und in den Zügen seines Antlitzes den Generalbaß studieren. Ich aber lebte noch in dem Traum der vorigen Nacht, den ich nicht aus meiner Seele verscheuchen konnte. Es war das alte Märchen, wie ein Ritter hinab steigt in einen tiefen Brunnen, wo unten die schönste Prinzessin zu einem starren Zauber-schlafe verwünscht ist. Ich selbst war der Ritter, und der Brunnen die dunkle Klausthaler Grube, und plötzlich erschienen viele Lichter, aus allen Seitenlöchern stürzten die wachsamen Zwerg-lein, schnitten zornige Gesichter, hieben nach mir mit ihren kurzen Schwertern, bliesen gellend ins Horn, daß immer mehr und mehre herzu eilten, und es wackelten entsetzlich ihre breiten Häupter. Wie ich darauf zuschlug und das Blut heraus floß, merkte ich erst, daß es die rotblühenden, langbärtigen Distelköpfe waren, die ich den Tag vorher an der Landstraße mit dem Stocke abgeschlagen hatte. Da waren sie auch gleich alle verscheucht, und ich gelangte in einen hellen Prachtsaal; in der Mitte stand, weiß verschleiert, und wie eine Bildsäule starr und regungslos, die Herzgeliebte, und ich küßte ihren Mund, und, beim lebendigen Gott! ich fühlte den beseligenden Hauch ihrer Seele und das süße Beben der lieblichen Lippen. Es war mir, als hörte ich, wie Gott rief: »Es werde·Licht!« blendend schoß herab ein Strahl des ewigen Lichts; aber in demselben Augenblick wurde es wieder Nacht, und alles rann chaotisch zusammen in ein wildes, wüstes Meer. Ein wildes, wüstes

upon many a lovely meadow vale. Silver waters rippled and rustled, sweet wood birds sang, the bells of the flocks tinkled, the many-shaded green trees were gilded by the sun, and over all the blue silk canopy of Heaven was so transparent that I could look through the depths even to the Holy of Holies, where angels sat at the feet of God, studying sublime thorough-bass in the features of the eternal countenance. But I was all the time lost in a dream of the previous night, which I could not banish. It was an echo of the old legend, how a knight descended into a deep fountain, beneath which the fairest princess of the world lay buried in a deathlike magic slumber. I myself was the knight, and the dark mine of Klausthal was the fountain. Suddenly, innumerable lights gleamed around me, wakeful dwarfs leapt from every cranny in the rocks, grimacing angrily, cutting at me with their short swords, blowing terribly on horns, which ever summoned more and more of their comrades, and frantically nodding their great heads. But as I hewed them down with my sword, and the blood flowed, I for the first time remarked that they were not really dwarfs, but the red-blooming long-bearded thistle tops, which I had the day before hewed down on the highway with my stick. At last they all vanished and I came to a splendid lighted hall, in the midst of which stood my heart's loved one, veiled in white and immovable as a statue. I kissed her mouth, and then—oh Heavens!—I felt the blessed breath of her soul and the sweet tremor of her lovely lips. It seemed that I heard the divine command, "Let there be light!" and a dazzling flash of eternal light shot down, but at the same instant it was again night, and all ran chaotically together into a wild desolate sea! A wild desolate sea! over whose foaming waves the ghosts of the departed madly chased each other, the white shrouds floating on the wind, while behind all, goading them on with cracking whip, ran a many-colored harlequin—and I was the

Meer! über das gärende Wasser jagten ängstlich die Gespenster der Verstorbenen, ihre weißen Totenhemde flatterten im Winde, hinter ihnen her, hetzend, mit klatschender Peitsche lief ein buntscheckiger Harlekin, und dieser war ich selbst – und plötzlich aus den dunkeln Wellen reckten die Meerungetüme ihre mißgestalteten Häupter, und langten nach mir mit ausgebreiteten Krallen, und vor Entsetzen erwacht ich. Wie doch zuweilen die allerschönsten Märchen verdorben werden! Eigentlich muß der Ritter, wenn er die schlafende Prinzessin gefunden hat, ein Stück aus ihrem kostbaren Schleier heraus schneiden; und wenn durch seine Kühnheit ihr Zauberschlaf gebrochen ist, und sie wieder in ihrem Palast auf dem goldenen Stuhle sitzt, muß der Ritter zu ihr treten und sprechen: Meine allerschönste Prinzessin, kennst du mich? Und dann antwortet sie: Mein allertapferster Ritter, ich kenne dich nicht. Und dieser zeigt ihr alsdann das aus ihrem Schleier heraus geschnittene Stück, das just in denselben wieder hineinpaßt, und beide umarmen sich zärtlich, und die Trompeter blasen, und die Hochzeit wird gefeiert.

Es ist wirklich ein eigenes Mißgeschick, daß meine Liebesträume selten ein so schönes Ende nehmen.

Der Name Goslar klingt so erfreulich, und es knüpfen sich daran so viele uralte Kaisererinnerungen, daß ich eine imposante, stattliche Stadt erwartete. Aber so geht es, wenn man die Berühmten in der Nähe besieht! Ich fand ein Nest mit meistens schmalen, labyrinthisch krummen Straßen, allwo mittendurch ein kleines Wasser, wahrscheinlich die Gose, fließt, verfallen und dumpfig, und ein Pflaster, so holprig wie Berliner Hexameter. Nur die Altertümlichkeiten der Einfassung, nämlich Reste von Mauern, Türmen und Zinnen, geben der Stadt etwas Pikantes. Einer dieser Türme, der Zwinger genannt, hat so dicke Mauern, daß ganze Gemächer darin ausgehauen sind. Der Platz vor der Stadt, wo der weitberühmte Schützenhof gehalten wird, ist eine schöne große Wiese, ringsum hohe Berge.

harlequin. Suddenly from the black waves the sea-monsters raised their misshapen heads, and yawned towards me with extended jaws, and I awoke in terror.

Alas! how the finest dreams may be spoiled! The knight, in fact, when he has found the lady, ought to cut a piece from her priceless veil, and after she has recovered from her magic sleep and sits again in glory in her hall, he should approach her and say, "My fairest princess, dost thou not know me? Then she will answer, "My bravest knight, I know thee not." And then he shows her the piece cut from her veil, exactly fitting the deficiency, and she knows that he is her deliverer, and both tenderly embrace, and the trumpets sound, and the marriage is celebrated!

It is really a very peculiar misfortune that my love dreams so seldom have so fine a conclusion.

The name of Goslar rings so pleasantly, and there are so many very ancient and imperial associations connected therewith,[49] that I had hoped to find an imposing and stately town. But it is always the same old story when we examine celebrities too closely! I found a nest of houses, drilled in every direction with narrow streets of labyrinthine crookedness, and amid them a miserable stream, probably the Goslar, winds its flat and melancholy way. The pavement of the town is as ragged as Berlin hexameters.[50] Only the antiquities which are embedded in the frame, or mounting, of the city; that is to say, its remnants of walls, towers, and battlements give the place a piquant look. One of these towers, known as the Zwinger, or donjon keep, has walls of such extraordinary thickness, that entire rooms are excavated therein. The open place before the town, where the world-renowned shooting-matches are held, is a beautiful large plain surrounded by high mountains. The market is small, and in its midst is a spring fountain, the water from which pours into a great metallic

Der Markt ist klein, in der Mitte steht ein Springbrunnen, dessen Wasser sich in ein großes Metallbecken ergießt. Bei Feuersbrünsten wird einige Mal daran geschlagen; es gibt dann einen weitschallenden Ton. Man weiß nichts vom Ursprunge dieses Beckens. Einige sagen, der Teufel habe es einst, zur Nachtzeit, dort auf den Markt hingestellt. Damals waren die Leute noch dumm, und der Teufel war auch dumm, und sie machten sich wechselseitig Geschenke. Das Rathaus zu Goslar ist eine weißangestrichene Wachtstube. Das daneben stehende Gildenhaus hat schon ein besseres Ansehen. Ungefähr von der Erde und vom Dach gleich weit entfernt stehen da die Standbilder deutscher Kaiser, räucherig schwarz und zum Teil vergoldet, in der einen Hand das Szepter, in der andern die Weltkugel; sehen aus wie gebratene Universitätspedelle. Einer dieser Kaiser hält ein Schwert, statt des Szepters. Ich konnte nicht erraten, was dieser Unterschied sagen soll; und es hat doch gewiß seine Bedeutung, da die Deutschen die merkwürdige Gewohnheit haben, daß sie bei allem, was sie tun, sich auch etwas denken.

In Gottschalks »Handbuch« hatte ich von dem uralten Dom und von dem berühmten Kaiserstuhl zu Goslar viel gelesen. Als ich aber beides besehen wollte, sagte man mir: der Dom sei niedergerissen und der Kaiserstuhl nach Berlin gebracht worden. Wir leben in einer bedeutungsschweren Zeit: tausendjährige Dome werden abgebrochen, und Kaiserstühle in die Rumpelkammer geworfen.

Einige Merkwürdigkeiten des seligen Doms sind jetzt in der Stephanskirche aufgestellt. Glasmalereien, die wunderschön sind, einige schlechte Gemälde, worunter auch ein Lukas Cranach sein soll, ferner ein hölzerner Christus am Kreuz, und ein heidnischer Opferaltar aus unbekanntem Metall; er hat die Gestalt einer länglich viereckigen Lade, und wird von vier Karyatiden getragen, die, in geduckter Stellung, die Hände stützend über dem Kopfe halten, und unerfreulich häßliche

basin. When an alarm of fire is raised, they strike strongly on this cup-formed basin, which gives out a very loud vibration. Nothing is known of the origin of this work. Some say that the devil placed it once during the night on the spot where it stands. In those days people were as yet fools, nor was the devil any wiser, and they mutually exchanged gifts.

The town hall of Goslar is a whitewashed police station. The Guildhall, hard by, has a somewhat better appearance. In this building, equidistant from roof and ceiling, stand the statues of the German emperors. Partly gilded, and altogether of a smoke-black hue, they look, with their scepters and globes of empire, like roasted college beadles. One of the emperors holds a sword, instead of a scepter. I cannot imagine the reason of this variation from the established order, though it has doubtless some occult signification, as Germans have the remarkable peculiarity of meaning something in whatever they do.

In Gottschalk's "Handbook," I had read much of the very ancient Dom, or Cathedral, and of the far-famed imperial throne at Goslar.[51] But when I wished to see these curiosities, I was informed that the church had been torn down, and that the throne had been carried to Berlin. We live in deeply significant times, when millennial churches are shattered to fragments, and imperial thrones are tumbled into the lumber-room.

A few memorials of the late cathedral of happy memory are still preserved in the church of St. Stephen. These consist of stained-glass pictures of great beauty, a few indifferent paintings, including a Lucas Cranach, a wooden Christ crucified, and a heathen altar of some unknown metal. This latter resembles a long square box, and is supported by four caryatids, which in a bowed position hold their hands over their heads, and make the most hideous grimaces. But far more hideous is the adjacent wooden crucifix of which I have just spoken. This head of

Gesichter schneiden. Indessen noch unerfreulicher ist das dabeistehende, schon erwähnte große hölzerne Kruzifix. Dieser Christuskopf, mit natürlichen Haaren und Dornen und blutbeschmiertem Gesichte, zeigt freilich höchst meisterhaft das Hinsterben eines Menschen, aber nicht eines gottgebornen Heilands. Nur das materielle Leiden ist in dieses Gesicht hinein geschnitzelt, nicht die Poesie des Schmerzes. Solch Bild gehört eher in einen antomischen Lehrsaal als in ein Gotteshaus.

Ich logierte in einem Gasthofe nahe dem Markte, wo mir das Mittagessen noch besser geschmeckt haben würde, hätte sich nur nicht der Herr Wirt mit seinem langen, überflüssigen Gesichte und seinen langweiligen Fragen zu mir hin gesetzt; glücklicher Weise ward ich bald erlöst durch die Ankunft eines andern Reisenden, der dieselben Fragen in derselben Ordnung aushalten mußte: quis? quid? ubi? quibus auxiliis? cur? quomodo? quando? Dieser Fremde war ein alter, müder, abgetragener Mann, der, wie aus seinen Reden hervorging, die ganze Welt durchwandert, besonders lang auf Batavia gelebt, viel Geld erworben und wieder alles verloren hatte, und jetzt, nach dreißigjähriger Abwesenheit, nach Quedlinburg, seiner Vaterstadt, zurückkehrte, – »denn«, setzte er hinzu, »unsere Familie hat dort ihr Erbbegräbnis«. Der Herr Wirt machte die sehr aufgeklärte Bemerkung: daß es doch für die Seele gleichgültig sei, wo unser Leib begraben wird. »Haben Sie es schriftlich?« antwortete der Fremde, und dabei zogen sich unheimlich schlaue Ringe um seine kümmerlichen Lippen und verblichenen Äugelein. »Aber«, setzte er ängstlich begütigend hinzu, »ich will darum über fremde Gräber doch nichts Böses gesagt haben; – die Türken begraben ihre Toten noch weit schöner als wir, ihre Kirchhöfe sind ordentlich Gärten, und da sitzen sie auf ihren weißen, beturbanten Grabsteinen, unter dem Schatten einer Zypresse, und streichen ihre ernsthaften Bärte, und rauchen ruhig ihren türkischen Tabak, aus ihren langen türkischen Pfeifen; – und bei den Chinesen gar ist es eine ordent-

Christ, with its real hair and thorns and blood-stained countenance, represents, in the most masterly manner, the death 'of a
man—but not of a divinely born Savior. Nothing but physical
suffering is portrayed in this image—not the sublime poetry of
pain. Such a work would be more appropriately placed in a hall
of anatomy than in a house of the Lord.

I lodged in a tavern, near the market, where I should have
enjoyed my dinner much better, if the landlord with his long,
superfluous face, and his still longer questions, had not planted
himself opposite to me. Fortunately I was soon relieved by the
arrival of another stranger, who was obliged to run in turn the
gantlet of *quis? quid? ubi? quibus auxiliis? cur? quomodo? quando?*[52] This stranger was an old, weary, wornout man, who, as it
appeared from his conversation, had been all over the world,
had resided very long in Batavia, had made much money, and
lost it all, and who now after thirty years' absence was returning
to Quedlinberg, his native city—"for," said he, "our family has
there its hereditary tomb." The landlord here made the highly
intelligent remark that it was all the same thing to the soul,
where the body was buried. "Have you scriptural authority
for that?" retorted the stranger, while mysterious and crafty
wrinkles circled around his pinched lips and faded eyes. "But,"
he added, as if nervously desirous of conciliating, "I mean no
harm against graves in foreign lands—oh, no!—the Turks bury
their dead more beautifully than we ours; their churchyards are
perfect gardens, and there they sit by their white turbaned
gravestones under cypress trees, and stroke their grave beards,
and calmly smoke their Turkish tobacco from their long Turkish
pipes; and then among the Chinese, it is a real pleasure to see
how genteelly they walk around, and pray, and drink tea
among the graves of their ancestors and how beautifully they
bedeck the beloved tombs with all sorts of gilt lacquered work,

49

liche Lust zuzusehen, wie sie auf den Ruhestätten ihrer Toten
manierlich herumtänzeln, und beten, und Tee trinken, und die
Geige spielen, und die geliebten Gräber gar hübsch zu verzieren
wissen mit allerlei vergoldetem Lattenwerk, Porzellanfigürchen,
Fetzen von buntem Seidenzeug, künstlichen Blumen, und
farbigen Laternchen – alles sehr hübsch – wie weit hab ich noch
bis Quedlinburg?«
Der Kirchhof in Goslar hat mich nicht sehr angesprochen.
Desto mehr aber jenes wunderschöne Lockenköpfchen, das bei
meiner Ankunft in der Stadt aus einem etwas hohen Parterre-
fenster lächelnd heraus schaute. Nach Tische suchte ich wieder
das liebe Fenster; aber jetzt stand dort nur ein Wasserglas mit
weißen Glockenblümchen. Ich kletterte hinauf, nahm die
artigen Blümchen aus dem Glase, steckte sie ruhig auf meine
Mütze, und kümmerte mich wenig um die aufgesperrten
Mäuler, versteinerten Nasen und Glotzaugen, womit die Leute
auf der Straße, besonders die alten Weiber, diesem qualifizierten
Diebstahle zusahen. Als ich eine Stunde später an demselben
Hause vorbei ging, stand die Holde am Fenster, und wie sie die
Glockenblümchen auf meiner Mütze gewahrte, wurde sie
blutrot und stürzte zurück. Ich hatte jetzt das schöne Antlitz
noch genauer gesehen; es war eine süße, durchsichtige Ver-
körperung von Sommerabendhauch, Mondschein, Nachti-
gallenlaut und Rosenduft. – Später, als es ganz dunkel geworden, trat sie vor die Türe. Ich kam – ich näherte mich – sie
zieht sich langsam zurück in den dunkeln Hausflur – ich fasse
sie bei der Hand und sage: ich bin ein Liebhaber von schönen
Blumen und Küssen, und was man mir nicht freiwillig gibt,
das stehle ich – und ich küßte sie rasch – und wie sie entfliehen
will, flüstere ich beschwichtigend: morgen reis ich fort und
komme wohl nie wieder – und ich fühle den geheimen Wider-
druck der lieblichen Lippen und der kleinen Hände – und
lachend eile ich von hinnen. Ja, ich muß lachen, wenn ich be-
denke, daß ich unbewußt jene Zauberformel ausgesprochen,

porcelain images, bits of colored silk, fresh flowers and variegated lanterns—all very fine indeed how far is it yet to Quedlinberg?" The churchyard at Goslar did not appeal very strongly to my feelings. But a certain very pretty blond ringleted head which peeped smilingly from a parterre window did. After dinner I again took an observation of this fascinating window, but instead of a maiden, I beheld a vase containing white bellflowers. I clambered up, stole the flowers, put them neatly in my cap, and descended, unheeding the gaping mouths, petrified noses, and goggle eyes with which the street population, and especially the old women, regarded this qualified theft. As I, an hour later, passed by the same house, the beauty stood by the window, and as she saw the flowers in my cap, she blushed like a ruby, and started back. This time I had seen the beautiful face to better advantage; it was a sweet transparent incarnation of summer evening air, moonshine, nightingale notes and rose perfume. Later—in the twilight hour, she was standing at the door. I came—I drew near—she slowly retreated into the dark entry—I followed, and seizing her band, said, "I am a lover of beautiful flowers and of kisses, and when they are not given to me, I steal them." Here I quickly snatched a kiss, and as she was about to fly, I whispered apologetically, "To-morrow I leave this town and never return again." Then I perceived a faint pressure of the lovely lips and of the little hand, and I — went smiling away. Yes, I must smile when I reflect that this was precisely the magic formula by which our red-and blue-coated cavaliers more frequently win female hearts, than by their mustachioed attractiveness. "To-morrow I leave, and never return again!"

My chamber commanded a fine view toward Rammelsberg. It was a lovely evening. Night was out hunting on her black steed, and the long cloud mane fluttered on the wind. I stood at my

wodurch unsere Rot- und Blauröcke, öfter als durch ihre schnurrbärtige Liebenswürdigkeit, die Herzen der Frauen bezwingen: »Ich reise morgen fort und komme wohl nie wieder!« Mein Logis gewährte eine herrliche Aussicht nach dem Rammelsberg. Es war ein schöner Abend. Die Nacht jagte auf ihrem schwarzen Rosse, und die langen Mähnen flatterten im Winde. Ich stand am Fenster und betrachtete den Mond. Gibt es wirklich einen Mann im Monde? Die Slawen sagen, er heiße Clotar, und das Wachsen des Mondes bewirke er durch Wasseraufgießen. Als ich noch klein war, hatte ich gehört: der Mond sei eine Frucht, die, wenn sie reif geworden, vom lieben Gott abgepflückt, und, zu den übrigen Vollmonden, in den großen Schrank gelegt werde, der am Ende der Welt steht, wo sie mit Brettern zugenagelt ist. Als ich größer wurde, bemerkte ich, daß die Welt nicht so eng begrenzt ist, und daß der menschliche Geist die hölzernen Schranken durchbrochen, und mit einem riesigen Petri-Schlüssel, mit der Idee der Unsterblichkeit, alle sieben Himmel aufgeschlossen hat. Unsterblichkeit! schöner Gedanke! wer hat dich zuerst erdacht? War es ein Nürnberger Spießbürger, der, mit weißer Nachtmütze auf dem Kopfe und weißer Tonpfeife im Maule, am lauen Sommerabend vor seiner Haustüre saß, und recht behaglich meinte: es wäre doch hübsch, wenn er nun so immer fort, ohne daß sein Pfeifchen und sein Lebensatemchen ausgingen, in die liebe Ewigkeit hineinvegetieren könnte! Oder war es ein junger Liebender, der in den Armen seiner Geliebten jenen Unsterblichkeitsgedanken dachte, und ihn dachte, weil er ihn fühlte, und weil er nichts anders fühlen und denken konnte! – Liebe! Unsterblichkeit! – in meiner Brust ward es plötzlich so heiß, daß ich glaubte, die Geographen hätten den Äquator verlegt, und er laufe jetzt gerade durch mein Herz. Und aus meinem Herzen ergossen sich die Gefühle der Liebe, ergossen sich sehnsüchtig in die weite Nacht. Die Blumen im Garten unter meinem Fenster

window watching the moon. Is there really a "man in the moon"? The Slavonians assert that there is such a being named Clotar,[53] and he causes the moon to grow by watering it. When I was little they told me that the moon was a fruit, and that when it was ripe, it was picked and laid away, amid a vast collection of old full moons, in a great bureau, which stood at the end of the world, where it is nailed up with boards. As I grew older, I remarked that the world was not by any means so limited as I had supposed it to be, and that human intelligence had broken up the wooden bureau, and with a terrible Hand of Glory had opened all the seven heavens. Immortality—dazzling idea! who first imagined thee! Was it some jolly burgher of Nuremburg, who with nightcap on his head, and white clay pipe in mouth, sat on some pleasant summer evening before his door, and reflected in all his comfort, that it would be right pleasant, if, with unextinguishable pipe, and endless breath, he could thus vegetate onwards for a blessed eternity ? Or was it a lover, who in the arms of his loved one thought the immortality thought, and that because he could think and feel naught beside!— Love! Immortality! It speedily became so hot in my breast, that I thought the geographers had misplaced the equator, and that it now ran directly through my heart. And from my heart poured out the feeling of love—it poured forth with wild longing into the broad night. The flowers in the garden beneath my window breathed a stronger perfume. Perfumes are the feelings of flowers, and as the human heart feels most powerful emotions in the night, when it believes itself to be alone and unperceived, so also do the flowers, soft-minded, yet ashamed, appear to await for concealing darkness, that they may give themselves wholly up to their feelings, and breathe them out in sweet odors. Pour forth, ye perfumes of my heart, and seek beyond yon blue mountain for the loved one of my dreams! Now she

dufteten stärker. Düfte sind die Gefühle der Blumen, und wie das Menschenherz in der Nacht, wo es sich einsam und unbelauscht glaubt, stärker fühlt, so scheinen auch die Blumen, sinnig verschämt, erst die umhüllende Dunkelheit zu erwarten, um sich gänzlich ihren Gefühlen hinzugeben, und sie auszuhauchen in süßen Düften. – Ergießt Euch, Ihr Düfte meines Herzens! und sucht hinter jenen Bergen die Geliebte meiner Träume! Sie liegt jetzt schon und schläft; zu ihren Füßen knieen Engel, und wenn sie im Schlafe lächelt, so ist es ein Gebet, das die Engel nachbeten; in ihrer Brust liegt der Himmel mit allen seinen Seligkeiten, und wenn sie atmet, so bebt mein Herz in der Ferne; hinter den seidnen Wimpern ihrer Augen ist die Sonne untergegangen, und wenn sie die Augen wieder aufschlägt, so ist es Tag, und die Vögel singen, und die Herdenglöckchen läuten, und die Berge schimmern in ihren schmaragdenen Kleidern, und ich schnüre den Ranzen und wandre.

In jener Nacht, die ich in Goslar zubrachte, ist mir etwas höchst Seltsames begegnet. Noch immer kann ich nicht ohne Angst daran zurück denken. Ich bin von Natur nicht ängstlich, aber vor Geistern fürchte ich mich fast so sehr wie der Österreichische Beobachter. Was ist Furcht? Kommt sie aus dem Verstande oder aus dem Gemüt? Über diese Frage disputierte ich so oft mit dem Doktor Saul Ascher, wenn wir zu Berlin, im Café royal, wo ich lange Zeit meinen Mittagstisch hatte, zufällig zusammen trafen. Er behauptete immer: wir fürchten etwas, weil wir es durch Vernunftschlüsse für furchtbar erkennen. Nur die Vernunft sei eine Kraft, nicht das Gemüt. Während ich gut aß und gut trank, demonstrierte er mir fortwährend die Vorzüge der Vernunft. Gegen das Ende seiner Demonstration pflegte er oft nach seiner Uhr zu sehen, und immer schloß er damit: »Die Vernunft ist das höchste Prinzip!«– Vernunft! Wenn ich jetzt dieses Wort höre, so sehe ich noch immer den Doktor Saul Ascher mit seinen abstrakten Beinen, mit seinem engen, transzendentalgrauen Leibrock, und mit

lies in slumber, at her feet kneel angels, and if she smiles in sleep it is a prayer which angels repeat; in her breast is heaven with all its raptures, and as she breathes, my heart, though afar, throbs responsively. Behind the silken lids of her eyes the sun has gone down, and when they are raised, the sun rises, and birds sing, and the bells of the flock tinkle, and I strap on my knapsack and depart.

During the night which I passed at Goslar a remarkably curious occurrence befell me. Even now, I cannot think of it without terror. I am not by nature cowardly, but I fear ghosts almost as much as the *Austrian Observer*.[54] What is fear? Does it come from the understanding or from the natural disposition? This was a point which I frequently disputed with Doctor Saul Ascher,[55] when we accidentally met in the Café Royal, in Berlin, where I for a long time dined. The doctor invariably maintained, that we feared anything, because we recognized it as fearful, owing to certain determinate conclusions of the reason. Only the reason was an active power—not the disposition. While I ate and drank to my heart's content, the doctor demonstrated to me the advantages of reason. Towards the end of his dissertation, he was accustomed to look at his watch and remark conclusively, "Reason is the highest principle!" Reason! Never do I hear this word without recalling Doctor Saul Ascher, with his abstract legs, his tight-fitting transcendental gray long coat, and his immovably icy face, which resembled a confused amalgam of geometrical problems. This man, deep in the fifties, was a personified straight line. In his striving for the positive, the poor man had philosophized everything beautiful out of existence, and with it everything like sunshine, religion and flowers, so that there remained nothing for him but a cold positive grave. The Apollo Belvedere and Christianity were the two especial objects of his malice, and he had even published a pamphlet against the

seinem schroffen, frierend kalten Gesichte, das einem Lehrbuche
der Geometrie als Kupfertafel dienen konnte. Dieser Mann, tief
in den Funfzigern, war eine personifizierte grade Linie. In
seinem Streben nach dem Positiven hatte der arme Mann sich
alles Herrliche aus dem Leben heraus philosophiert, alle
Sonnenstrahlen, allen Glauben und alle Blumen, und es blieb
ihm nichts übrig, als das kalte, positive Grab. Auf den Apoll
von Belvedere und auf das Christentum hatte er eine spezielle
Malice. Gegen letzteres schrieb er sogar eine Broschüre, worin
er dessen Unvernünftigkeit und Unhaltbarkeit bewies. Er hat
überhaupt eine ganze Menge Bücher geschrieben, worin immer
die Vernunft von ihrer eigenen Vortrefflichkeit renommiert,
und wobei es der arme Doktor gewiß ernsthaft genug meinte,
und also in dieser Hinsicht alle Achtung verdiente. Darin aber
bestand ja eben der Hauptspaß, daß er ein so ernsthaft närrisches
Gesicht schnitt, wenn er dasjenige nicht begreifen konnte, was
jedes Kind begreift, eben weil es ein Kind ist. Einige Mal besuchte ich auch den Vernunftdoktor in seinem eigenen Hause,
wo ich schöne Mädchen bei ihm fand; denn die Vernunft ver-
bietet nicht die Sinnlichkeit. Als ich ihn einst ebenfalls besuchen
wollte, sagte mir sein Bedienter: der Herr Doktor ist eben gestorben. Ich fühlte nicht viel mehr dabei, als wenn er gesagt
hätte: der Herr Doktor ist ausgezogen.

Doch zurück nach Goslar. »Das höchste Prinzip ist die Vernunft!« sagte ich beschwichtigend zu mir selbst, als ich ins Bett
stieg. Indessen, es half nicht. Ich hatte eben in Varnhagen von
Enses »Deutsche Erzählungen«, die ich von Clausthal mit-
genommen hatte, jene entsetzliche Geschichte gelesen, wie der
Sohn, den sein eigener Vater ermorden wollte, in der Nacht von
dem Geiste seiner toten Mutter gewarnt wird. Die wunderbare
Darstellung dieser Geschichte bewirkte, daß mich während
des Lesens ein inneres Grauen durchfröstelte. Auch erregen
Gespenstererzählungen ein noch schauerlicheres Gefühl, wenn
man sie auf der Reise liest, und zumal des Nachts, in einer Stadt,

latter, in which he had demonstrated its unreasonableness and untenableness. In addition to this, he had, however, written a great number of books, in all of which Reason shone, forth in all its peculiar excellence, and as the poor doctor meant what he said in all seriousness, they were, so far, deserving of respect. But the great joke consisted precisely in this, that the doctor invariably cut such a seriously absurd figure in not comprehending that which every child comprehends, simply because it is a child. I visited the doctor several times in his own house, where I found him in company with very pretty girls, for Reason, it seems, however abstract, does not prohibit the enjoyment of the things of this world. Once, however, when I called, his servant told me that the Herr Doctor had just died. I experienced as much emotion on this occasion, as if I had been told that the Herr Doctor had just stepped out.

To return to Goslar. "The highest principle is Reason," said I consolingly to myself as I slid into bed. But it availed me nothing. I had just been reading in Varnhagen von Ense's *German Narrations*,[56] which I had brought with me from Klausthal, that terrible tale of a son, who, when about to murder his father, was warned in the night by the ghost of his mother. The wonderful truthfulness with which this story is depicted, caused while reading it a shudder of horror in all my veins. Ghost stories invariably thrill us with additional horror when read during a journey, and by night in a town, in a house, and in a chamber where we have never before been. We involuntarily reflect, "How many horrors may have been perpetrated on this very spot where I now lie?" Meanwhile, the moon shone into my room in a doubtful, suspicious manner; all kinds of uncalled-for shapes quivered on the walls, and I laid me down and glanced fearfully around, I beheld. . . .

in einem Hause, in einem Zimmer, wo man noch nie gewesen.
Wie viel Gräßliches mag sich schon zugetragen haben auf
diesem Flecke, wo du eben liegst? so denkt man unwillkürlich.
Überdies schien jetzt der Mond so zweideutig ins Zimmer
herein, an der Wand bewegten sich allerlei unberufene Schatten, and als ich mich im Bett aufrichtete, um hin zu sehen, erblickte ich –
Es gibt nichts Unheimlicheres, als wenn man, bei Mondschein, das eigene Gesicht zufällig im Spiegel sieht. In demselben Augenblicke schlug eine schwerfällige, gähnende Glocke,
und zwar so lang und langsam, daß ich nach dem zwölften
Glockenschlage sicher glaubte, es seien unterdessen volle
zwölf Stunden verflossen, und es müßte wieder von vorn an-
fangen, zwölf zu schlagen. Zwischen dem vorletzten und
letzten Glockenschlage schlug noch eine andere Uhr, sehr rasch,
fast keifend gell, und vielleicht ärgerlich über die Langsamkeit
ihrer Frau Gevatterin. Als beide eiserne Zungen schwiegen,
und tiefe Todesstille im ganzen Hause herrschte, war es mir
plötzlich, als hörte ich auf dem Korridor, vor meinem Zimmer,
etwas schlottern und schlappen, wie der unsichere Gang eines
alten Mannes. Endlich öffnete sich meine Tür, und langsam trat
herein der verstorbene Doktor Saul Ascher. Ein kaltes Fieber
rieselte mir durch Mark und Bein, ich zitterte wie Espenlaub,
und kaum wagte ich das Gespenst anzusehen. Er sah aus wie
sonst, derselbe transzendentalgraue Leibrock, dieselben abstrakten Beine, und dasselbe mathematische Gesicht; nur
war dieses etwas gelblicher als sonst, auch der Mund, der sonst
zwei Winkel von $22^1/_2$ Grad bildete, war zusammengekniffen,
und die Augenkreise hatten einen größeren Radius. Schwan-
kend, und wie sonst sich auf sein spanisches Röhrchen stützend,
näherte er sich mir, und in seinem gewöhnlichen mundfaulen
Dialekte sprach er freundlich: »Fürchten Sie sich nicht, und
glauben Sie nicht, daß ich ein Gespenst sei. Es ist Täuschung
Ihrer Phantasie, wenn Sie mich als Gespenst zu sehen glauben.

There is nothing so uncanny as when a man sees his own face by moonlight in a mirror. At the same instant there struck a deep booming, yawning bell, and that so slowly and wearily that I firmly believed that it had been full twelve hours striking, and that it was now time to begin over again. Between the last and next to the last tones, there struck in very abruptly, as if irritated and scolding, another bell, who was apparently out of patience with the slowness of her friend. As the two iron tongues were silenced, and the stillness of death sank over the whole house, I suddenly seemed to bear, in the corridor before my chamber, something halting and waddling along, like the unsteady steps of a man. At last he door slowly opened, and there entered deliberately the late departed Doctor Saul Ascher. A cold fever drizzled through marrow and vein—I trembled like an ivy leaf, and scarcely dared I gaze upon the ghost. He appeared as usual, with the same transcendental gray long coat, the same abstract legs, and the same mathematical face; only this latter was a little yellower than usual, and the mouth, which formerly described two angles of 22 ½ degrees, was pinched together, and the circles around the eyes had a somewhat greater radius. Tottering, and supporting himself as usual upon his Malacca cane, he approached me, and said, in his usual drawling dialect, but in a friendly manner: "Do not be afraid, nor believe that I am a ghost. It is a deception of your imagination, if you believe that you see me as a ghost. What is a ghost? Define one. Deduce for me the conditions of the possibility of a ghost. In what reasonable connection does such an apparition coincide with reason itself? Reason, I say, reason! Here the ghost proceeded to analyze reason, cited from Kant's *Critique of Pure Reason,* part 2, 1st section, chap. 3,[57] the distinction between phenomena and noumena, then proceeded

Was ist ein Gespenst? Geben Sie mir eine Definition? Dedu-
zieren Sie mir die Bedingungen der Möglichkeit eines Ge-
spenstes? In welchem vernünftigen Zusammenhange stände
eine solche Erscheinung mit der Vernunft? Die Vernunft, ich
sage die Vernunft –« Und nun schritt das Gespenst zu einer
Analyse der Vernunft, zitierte Kants »Kritik der reinen Vernunft«, 2ter Teil, 1ster Abschnitt 2tes Buch, 3tes Hauptstück, die
Unterscheidung von Phänomena und Noumena, konstruierte
alsdann den problematischen Gespensterglauben, setzte einen
Syllogismus auf den andern, und schloß mit dem logischen
Beweise: daß es durchaus keine Gespenster gibt. Mir unterdessen lief der kalte Schweiß über den Rücken, meine Zähne
klapperten wie Kastagnetten, aus Seelenangst nickte ich un-
bedingte Zustimmung bei jedem Satz, womit der spukende
Doktor die Absurdität aller Gespensterfurcht bewies, und derselbe demonstrierte so eifrig, daß er einmal in der Zerstreuung,
statt seiner goldenen Uhr, eine Hand voll Würmer aus der Uhr-
tasche zog, und seinen Irrtum bemerkend, mit possierlich
ängstlicher Hastigkeit wieder einsteckte. »Die Vernunft ist das
höchste –« da schlug die Glocke Eins und das Gespenst ver-
schwand.

Von Goslar ging ich den andern Morgen weiter, halb auf
Geratewohl, halb in der Absicht, den Bruder des Klausthaler
Bergmanns aufzusuchen. Wieder schönes, liebes Sonntagswetter.
Ich bestieg Hügel und Berge, betrachtete, wie die Sonne den
Nebel zu verscheuchen suchte, wanderte freudig durch die
schauernden Wälder, und um mein träumendes Haupt klingelten die Glockenblümchen von Goslar. In ihren weißen Nacht-
mänteln standen die Berge, die Tannen rüttelten sich den Schlaf
aus den Gliedern, der frische Morgenwind frisierte ihnen die
herabhängenden, grünen Haare, die Vöglein hielten Betstunde,
das Wiesental blitzte wie eine diamantenbesäete Golddecke,
und der Hirt schritt darüber hin mit seiner läutenden Herde.
Ich mochte mich wohl eigentlich verirrt haben. Man schlägt

to construct a hypothetical system of ghosts, piled one syllogism on another, and concluded with the logical proof that there are absolutely no ghosts. Meanwhile the cold sweat beaded over me, my teeth clattered like castanets, and from very agony of soul I nodded an unconditional assent to every assertion which the phantom Doctor alleged against the absurdity of being afraid of ghosts, and which he demonstrated with such zeal, that finally, in a moment of abstraction, instead of his gold watch, he drew a handful of grave worms from his vest pocket, and remarking his error, replaced them with a ridiculous but terrified haste. "The reason is the highest—" Here the clock struck one, and the ghost vanished.

I wandered forth from Goslar the next morning, half at random, and half intending to visit the brother of the Klausthaler miner. I climbed hill and mount, saw how the sun strove to drive afar the mists, and wandered merrily through the trembling woods, while around my dreaming head rang the bell-flowers of Goslar. The mountains stood in their white night-robes, the fir-trees were shaking sleep out of their branching limbs, the fresh morning wind curled their down-drooping green locks, the birds were at morning prayers, the meadow vale flashed like a golden surface sprinkled with diamonds, and the shepherd passed over it with his bleating flock. I had gone astray. Men are ever striking out short cuts and by-paths, hoping to abridge their journey. It is in life as in the Harz. However, there are good souls everywhere to bring us again to the right way. This they do right willingly, appearing to take a particular satisfaction, to judge from their self-gratified air and benevolent tones, in pointing out to us the great wanderings which we have made from the right road, the abysses and morasses into which we might have sunk, and, finally, what a piece of good luck it was for us to encounter, betimes, people

immer Seitenwege und Fußsteige ein, und glaubt dadurch näher zum Ziele zu gelangen. Wie im Leben überhaupt, gehts uns auch auf dem Harze. Aber es gibt immer gute Seelen, die uns wieder auf den rechten Weg bringen; sie tun es gern, und finden noch obendrein ein besonderes Vergnügen daran, wenn sie uns mit selbstgefälliger Miene und wohlwollend lauter Stimme bedeuten: welche große Umwege wir gemacht, in welche Abgründe und Sümpfe wir versinken konnten, und welch ein Glück es sei, daß wir so wegkundige Leute, wie sie sind, noch zeitig angetroffen. Einen solchen Berichtiger fand ich unweit der Harzburg. Es war ein wohlgenährter Bürger von Goslar, ein glänzend wampiges, dummkluges Gesicht; er sah aus, als habe er die Viehseuche erfunden. Wir gingen eine Strecke zusammen, und er erzählte mir allerlei Spukgeschichten, die hübsch klingen konnten, wenn sie nicht alle darauf hinaus liefen, daß es doch kein wirklicher Spuk gewesen, sondern daß die weiße Gestalt ein Wilddieb war, und daß die wimmernden Stimmen von den eben geworfenen Jungen einer Bache (wilden Sau), und das Geräusch auf dem Boden von der Hauskatze herrührte. Nur wenn der Mensch krank ist, setzte er hinzu, glaubt er Gespenster zu sehen; was aber seine Wenigkeit anbelange, so sei er selten krank, nur zuweilen leide er an Hautübeln, und dann kuriere er sich jedesmal mit nüchternem Speichel. Er machte mich auch aufmerksam auf die Zweckmäßigkeit und Nützlichkeit in der Natur. Die Bäume sind grün, weil Grün gut für die Augen ist. Ich gab ihm Recht und fügte hinzu, daß Gott das Rindvieh erschaffen, weil Fleischsuppen den Menschen stärken, daß er die Esel erschaffen, damit sie dem Menschen zu Vergleichungen dienen können, und daß er den Menschen selbst erschaffen, damit er Fleischsuppen essen und kein Esel sein soll. Mein Begleiter war entzückt, einen Gleichgestimmten gefunden zu haben, sein Antlitz erglänzte noch freudiger, und bei dem Abschiede war er gerührt.

who knew the road as well as themselves. Such a guide-post I found not far from the Harzburg, in the person of a well-fed citizen of Goslar—a man of shining, double-chinned, slow cunning countenance, who looked as if he had discovered the murrain. We went along for some distance together, and he narrated many ghost stories, which would have all been well enough if they had not all concluded with an explanation that there was no real ghost in the case, but that the specter in white was a poacher, that the wailing sound was caused by the new-born farrow of a wild sow, and that the rapping and scraping on the roof was caused by cats. "Only when a man is sick," observed my guide, "does he ever believe that he sees ghosts"; and to this he added the remark, that as for his own humble self, he was but seldom sick—only at times a little wrong about the head, and that he invariably relieved this by dieting. He then called my attention to the appropriateness and use of all things in nature. Trees are green, because green is good for the eyes. I assented to this, adding that the Lord had made cattle because beef soup strengthened man, that jackasses were created for the purpose of serving as comparisons, and that man existed that he might eat beef soup, and realize that he was no jackass. My companion was delighted to meet with one of sympathetic views, his face glowed with a greater joy, and on parting from me he appeared to be sensibly moved.

As long as he was with me Nature seemed benumbed, but when he departed the trees began again to speak, the sunrays flashed, the meadow flowers danced once more, and the blue heavens embraced the green earth. Yes—I know better. God hath created man that he may admire the beauty and the glory of the world. Every author, be he ever so great, desires that his work may be praised. And in the Bible, that great memoir of

So lange er neben mir ging, war gleichsam die ganze Natur
entzaubert, sobald er aber fort war, fingen die Bäume wieder
an zu sprechen, und die Sonnenstrahlen erklangen und die
Wiesenblümchen tanzten, und der blaue Himmel umarmte die
grüne Erde. Ja, ich weiß es besser; Gott hat den Menschen
erschaffen, damit er die Herrlichkeit der Welt bewundere. Jeder
Autor, und sei er noch so groß, wünscht, daß sein Werk gelobt
werde. Und in der Bibel, den Memoiren Gottes, steht aus-
drücklich: daß er die Menschen erschaffen zu seinem Ruhm und
Preis.

Nach einem langen Hin- und Herwandern gelangte ich zu
der Wohnung des Bruders meines Clausthaler Freundes, über-
nachtete alldort, und erlebte folgendes schöne Gedicht:

I

Auf dem Berge steht die Hütte,
Wo der alte Bergmann wohnt;
Dorten rauscht die grüne Tanne,
Und erglänzt der goldne Mond.

In der Hütte steht ein Lehnstuhl,
Reich geschnitzt und wunderlich,
Der darauf sitzt, der ist glücklich,
Und der Glückliche bin Ich!

Auf dem Schemel sitzt die Kleine,
Stützt den Arm auf meinen Schoß;
Äuglein wie zwei blaue Sterne,
Mündlein wie die Purpurros.

Und die lieben, blauen Sterne
Schaun mich an so himmelgroß,
Und sie legt den Liljenfinger
Schalkhaft auf die Purpurros.

Nein, es sieht uns nicht die Mutter,
Denn sie spinnt mit großem Fleiß,

God, it is distinctly written that he hath made man for his own honor and praise.

After long wandering, here and there, I came to the dwelling of the brother of my Klausthaler friend. Here I stayed all night, and experienced the following beautiful poem:[58]

I

On yon rock the hut is standing,
Of the ancient mountaineer.
There the dark green fir-trees rustle,
And the moon is shining clear.

In the hut there stands an armchair
Which quaint carvings beautify;
He who sits therein is happy,
And that happy man am I.

On the footstool sits a maiden,
On my Iap her arms repose:
With her eyes like blue stars beaming,
And her mouth a new-born rose.

And the dear blue stars shine on me,
Full as heaven is their gaze;
And her little lily finger
Archly on the rose she lays.

"Nay—thy mother cannot see us,
For she spins the whole day long;

Und der Vater spielt die Zither,
Und er singt die alte Weis.

Und die Kleine flüstert leise,
Leise, mit gedämpftem Laut;
Manches wichtige Geheimnis
Hat sie mir schon anvertraut.

»Aber seit die Muhme tot ist,
Können wir ja nicht mehr gehn
Nach dem Schützenhof zu Goslar,
Und dort ist es gar zu schön.

Hier dagegen ist es einsam,
Auf der kalten Bergeshöh,
Und des Winters sind wir gänzlich
Wie vergraben in dem Schnee.

Und ich bin ein banges Mädchen,
Und ich fürcht mich wie ein Kind
Vor den bösen Bergesgeistern,
Die des Nachts geschäftig sind.«

Plötzlich schweigt die liebe Kleine,
Wie vom eignen Wort erschreckt,
Und sie hat mit beiden Händchen
Ihre Äugelein bedeckt.

Lauter rauscht die Tanne draußen,
Und das Spinnrad schnarrt und brummt,
Und die Zither klingt dazwischen,
Und die alte Weise summt:

»Fürcht dich nicht, du liebes Kindchen,
Vor der bösen Geister Macht;
Tag und Nacht, du liebes Kindchen,
Halten Englein bei dir Wacht!«

And thy father plays the cither
As he sings a good old song."

And the maiden softly whispers,
So that none around may hear:
Many a solemn little secret
Hath she murmured in my ear.

"Since I lost my aunt who loved me,
Now we never more repair
To the shooting-ground at Goslar,
And it is so pleasant there!

And up here it is so lonely
On the rocks where cold winds blow;
And in winter, we are ever
Deeply buried in the snow.

And I'm such a timid creature,
And I'm frightened like a child;
At the evil mountain spirits,
Who by night are raging wild."

At the thought the maid was silent,
As if terror thrilled her breast ;
And the small hands, white and dimpled
To her sweet blue eyes she pressed.

Loud, without, the fir-trees rustle,
Loud the spinning-wheel still rings:
And the cither sounds above them,
While the father softly sings.

"Dearest child—no evil spirits
Should have power to cause thee dread;
For good angels still are watching
Night and day around thy head."

II

Tannenbaum, mit grünen Fingern,
Pocht ans niedre Fensterlein,
Und der Mond, der gelbe Lauscher,
Wirft sein süßes Licht herein.

Vater, Mutter schnarchen leise
In dem nahen Schlafgemach,
Doch wir beide, selig schwatzend,
Halten uns einander wach.

»Daß du gar zu oft gebetet,
Das zu glauben wird mir schwer,
Jenes Zucken deiner Lippen
Kommt wohl nicht vom Beten her.

Jenes böse, kalte Zucken,
Das erschreckt mich jedesmal,
Doch die dunkle Angst beschwichtigt
Deiner Augen frommer Strahl.

Auch bezweifl ich, daß du glaubest,
Was so rechter Glauben heißt,
Glaubst wohl nicht an Gott den Vater,
An den Sohn und heilgen Geist?«

Ach, mein Kindchen, schon als Knabe,
Als ich saß auf Mutters Schoß,
Glaubte ich an Gott den Vater,
Der da waltet gut und groß;

Der die schöne Erd erschaffen,
Und die schönen Menschen drauf,
Der den Sonnen, Monden, Sternen
Vorgezeichnet ihren Lauf.

Als ich größer wurde, Kindchen,
Noch viel mehr begriff ich schon,
Und begriff, und ward vernünftig,
Und ich glaub auch an den Sohn;

II

Fir-tree with his dark green fingers
Taps upon the window low;
And the moon, a yellow listener,
Casts within her sweetest glow.

Father, mother, both are sleeping,
Near at hand their rest they take;
But we two in pleasant gossip,
Keep each other long awake.

"That thou prayest much too often,
Seems unlikely I declare;
On thy lips there's a contraction
Which was never born of prayer.

Ah, that heartless, cold expression
Terrifies me as I gaze;
Though a solemn sorrow darkens
In thine eyes, their gentle rays.

And I doubt if thou believest
What is held for truth by most;
Hast thou faith in God the Father
In the Son and Holy Ghost?"

Ah, my darling; when, an infant,
By my mother's knee I stood,
I believed in God the Father,
He who ruleth great and good.

He who made the world so lovely,
Gave man beauty, gave him force
And to sun and moon and planets,
Preappointed each their course.

As I older grew, my darling,
And my way in wisdom won;
I, in reason comprehended,
And believe now in the Son.

An den lieben Sohn, der liebend
Uns die Liebe offenbart,
Und zum Lohne, wie gebräuchlich,
Von dem Volk gekreuzigt ward.

Jetzo, da ich ausgewachsen,
Viel gelesen, viel gereist,
Schwillt mein Herz, und ganz von Herzen
Glaub ich an den heilgen Geist.

Dieser tat die größten Wunder,
Und viel größre tut er noch;
Er zerbrach die Zwingherrnburgen,
Und zerbrach des Knechtes Joch.

Alte Todeswunden heilt er,
Und erneut das alte Recht:
Alle Menschen, gleichgeboren,
Sind ein adliges Geschlecht.

Er verscheucht die bösen Nebel,
Und das dunkle Hirngespinst,
Das uns Lieb und Lust verleidet,
Tag und Nacht uns angegrinst.

Tausend Ritter, wohl gewappnet,
Hat der heilge Geist erwählt,
Seinen Willen zu erfüllen,
Und er hat sie mutbeseelt.

Ihre teuern Schwerter blitzen,
Ihre guten Banner wehn!
Ei, du möchtest wohl, mein Kindchen,
Solche stolze Ritter sehn?

Nun, so schau mich an, mein Kindchen,
Küsse mich und schaue dreist;
Denn ich selber bin ein solcher
Ritter von dem heilgen Geist.

In the well-loved Son, who loving,
Oped the gates of Love so wide;
And for thanks—as is the custom—
By the world was crucified.

Now, at man's estate arriving,
Full experience I boast;
And with heart expanded, truly
I believe in the Holy Ghost,

Who hath worked the greatest wonders,
Greater still he'll work again;
He hath broken tyrant's strongholds
And he breaks the vassal's chain.

Ancient deadly wounds he healeth,
He renews man's ancient right;
All to him, born free and equal,
Are as nobles in his sight.

Clouds of evil flee before him,
And those cobwebs of the brain,
Which forbade us love and pleasure,
Scowling grimly on our pain.

And a thousand knights well weaponed
Hath he chosen, and required
To fulfil his holy bidding,
All with noblest zeal inspired.

Lo ! their precious swords are gleaming,
And their banners wave in fight!
What! thou fain wouldst see, my darling,
Such a proud and noble knight?

Well, then gaze upon me, dearest,
I am of that lordly host.
Kiss me ! I am an elected
True knight of the Holy Ghost!"

III

Still versteckt der Mond sich draußen
Hinterm grünen Tannenbaum,
Und im Zimmer unsre Lampe
Flackert matt und leuchtet kaum.

Aber meine blauen Sterne
Strahlen auf in hellerm Licht,
Und es glüht die Purpurrose,
Und das liebe Mädchen spricht:

»Kleines Völkchen, Wichtelmännchen,
Stehlen unser Brot und Speck,
Abends liegt es noch im Kasten,
Und des Morgens ist es weg.

Kleines Völkchen, unsre Sahne
Nascht es von der Milch, und läßt
Unbedeckt die Schüssel stehen,
Und die Katze säuft den Rest.

Und die Katz ist eine Hexe,
Denn sie schleicht, bei Nacht und Sturm,
Drüben nach dem Geisterberge,
Nach dem altverfallnen Turm.

Dort hat einst ein Schloß gestanden,
Voller Lust und Waffenglanz;
Blanke Ritter, Fraun und Knappen
Schwangen sich im Fackeltanz.

Da verwünschte Schloß und Leute
Eine böse Zauberin,
Nur die Trümmer blieben stehen,
Und die Eulen nisten drin.

Doch die selge Muhme sagte:
Wenn man spricht das rechte Wort,
Nächtlich zu der rechten Stunde,
Drüben an dem rechten Ort:

III

Silently the moon goes hiding
Down behind the dark green trees;
And the lamp which lights our chamber
Flickers in the evening breeze.

But the star-blue eyes are beaming
Softly o'er the dimpled cheeks,
And the purple rose is gleaming,
While the gentle maiden speaks.

"Little people—fairy goblins—
Steal away our meat and bread;
In the chest it lies at evening,
In the morning it has fled.

From our milk, the little people
Steal the cream and all the best;
Then they leave the dish uncovered,
And our cat drinks up the rest.

And the cat's a witch, I'm certain,
For by night when storms arise;
Oft she glides to yonder Ghost-Rock,
Where the fallen tower lies.

There was once a splendid castle,
Home of joy and weapons bright;
Where there swept in stately torch dance,
lady, page, and arméd knight.

But a sorceress charmed the castle,
With its lords and ladies fair;
Now it is a lonely ruin,
And the owls are nestling there.

But my aunt hath often told me,
Could I speak the proper word,
In the proper place up yonder,
When the proper hour occurred,

So verwandeln sich die Trümmer
Wieder in ein helles Schloß,
Und es tanzen wieder lustig
Ritter, Fraun und Knappentroß;

Und wer jenes Wort gesprochen,
Dem gehören Schloß und Leut,
Pauken und Trompeten huldgen
Seiner jungen Herrlichkeit.«

Also blühen Märchenbilder
Aus des Mundes Röselein,
Und die Augen gießen drüber
Ihren blauen Sternenschein.

Ihre goldnen Haare wickelt
Mir die Kleine um die Händ,
Gibt den Fingern hübsche Namen,
Lacht und küßt, und schweigt am End.

Und im stillen Zimmer alles
Blickt mich an so wohlvertraut;
Tisch und Schrank, mir ist als hätt ich
Sie schon früher mal geschaut.

Freundlich ernsthaft schwatzt die Wanduhr,
Und die Zither, hörbar kaum,
Fängt von selber an zu klingen,
Und ich sitze wie im Traum.

Jetzo ist die rechte Stunde,
Und es ist der rechte Ort;
Ei, was gilts, mit kühnen Lippen
Sprech ich aus das rechte Wort

Siehst du schon, mein Kind, es dämmert
Und erbebt die Mitternacht,
Bach und Tannen brausen lauter,
Und der alte Berg erwacht.

Zitherklang und Zwergenlieder
Tönen aus des Berges Spalt,

Then the walls would change by magic
To a castle gleaming bright;
And I'd see in stately dances,
Dame and page and gallant knight.

He who speaks the word of power
Wins the castle for his own;
And the knights with drum and trumpet,
Loud will hail him lord alone."

Thus, sweet legendary pictures
From the little rose-mouth bloom;
And the gentle eyes are shedding
Star-blue luster through the gloom.

Round my hand the little maiden
Winds her gold locks as she will,
Gives a name to every finger,
Kisses—smiles, and then is still.

All things in the silent chamber
Seem at once familiar grown,
As if e'en the chairs and clothes-press,
Well, of old, to me were known.

Now the clock talks kindly, gravely,
And the cither, as 'twould seem,
Of itself is faintly chiming,
And I sit as in a dream.

Now the proper hour is o'er us,
Here's the place where't should be heard;
Child—how thou wouldst be astonished,
Should I speak the magic word!

If I spoke that word, then fading
Night would thrill in fearful strife;
Trees and streams would roar together
As the castle woke to life.

Ringing lutes and goblin ditties
From the clefted rock would sound;

Und es sprießt, wie 'n toller Frühling,
Draus hervor ein Blumenwald;

Blumen, kühne Wunderblumen,
Blätter, breit und fabelhaft,
Duftig bunt und hastig regsam,
Wie gedrängt von Leidenschaft.

Rosen, wild wie rote Flammen,
Sprühn aus dem Gewühl hervor;
Liljen, wie kristallne Pfeiler,
Schießen himmelhoch empor.

Und die Sterne, groß wie Sonnen,
Schaun herab mit Sehnsuchtglut;
In der Liljen Riesenkelche
Strömet ihre Strahlenflut.

Doch wir selber, süßes Kindchen,
Sind verwandelt noch viel mehr;
Fackelglanz und Gold und Seide
Schimmern lustig um uns her.

Du, du wurdest zur Prinzessin,
Diese Hütte ward zum Schloß,
Und da jubeln und da tanzen
Ritter, Fraun und Knappentroß.

Aber Ich, ich hab erworben
Dich und Alles, Schloß und Leut;
Pauken und Trompeten huldgen
Meiner jungen Herrlichkeit!

Die Sonne ging auf. Die Nebel flohen, wie Gespenster beim
dritten Hahnenschrei. Ich stieg wieder bergauf und bergab, und
vor mir schwebte die schöne Sonne, immer neue Schönheiten
beleuchtend. Der Geist des Gebirges begünstigte mich ganz
offenbar; er wußte wohl, daß so ein Dichtermensch viel Hüb-
sches wieder erzählen kann, und er ließ mich diesen Morgen

Like a mad and merry spring-tide
Flowers grow forest-high around.

Flowers—startling, wondrous flowers,
Leaves of vast and fabled form,
Strangely perfumed—wildly quivering,
As if thrilled with passion's storm.

Roses, wild as crimson flashes,
O'er the busy tumult rise
Giant lilies, white as crystal,
Shoot like columns to the skies.

Great as suns the stars above us
Gaze adown with burning glow;
In the lilies, giant calyx
All their floods of flashes flow.

We ourselves, my little maiden,
Would be changéd more than all;
Torchlight gleams, o'er gold and satin
Round us merrily would fall.

Thou thyself wouldst be the princess,
And this hut thy castle high;
Ladies, lords, and graceful pages,
Would be dancing, singing by.

I, however, I have conquered
Thee, and all things, with the word—
Serfs and castle—lo! with trumpet
Loud they hail me as their lord!

The sun rose. Clouds flitted away like phantoms at the third
crow of the cock. Again I wandered up, hill and down dale,
while overhead swept the fair sun, ever lighting up new scenes
of beauty. The Spirit of the Mountain evidently favored me,
well knowing that a poetical character has it in his power to say

seinen Harz sehen, wie ihn gewiß nicht jeder sah. Aber auch mich sah der Harz, wie mich nur wenige gesehen, in meinen Augenwimpern flimmerten eben so kostbare Perlen wie in den Gräsern des Tals. Morgentau der Liebe feuchtete meine Wangen, die rauschenden Tannen verstanden mich, ihre Zweige taten sich von einander, bewegten sich herauf und herab, gleich stummen Menschen, die mit den Händen ihre Freude bezeigen, und in der Ferne klangs wunderbar geheimnisvoll, wie Glockengeläute einer verlornen Waldkirche. Man sagt, das seien die Herdenglöckchen, die im Harz so lieblich, klar und rein gestimmt sind.

Nach dem Stand der Sonne war es Mittag, als ich auf eine solche Herde stieß, und der Hirt, ein freundlich blonder junger Mensch, sagte mir: der große Berg, an dessen Fuß ich stände, sei der alte, weltberühmte Brocken. Viele Stunden ringsum liegt kein Haus, und ich war froh genug, daß mich der junge Mensch einlud, mit ihm zu essen. Wir setzten uns nieder zu einem Dejeuner dinatoire, das aus Käse und Brot bestand; die Schäfchen erhaschten die Krumen, die lieben, blanken Kühlein sprangen um uns herum, und klingelten schelmisch mit ihren Glöckchen, und lachten uns an mit ihren großen, vergnügten Augen. Wir tafelten recht königlich; überhaupt schien mir mein Wirt ein echter König, und weil er bis jetzt der einzige König ist, der mir Brot gegeben hat, so will ich ihn auch königlich besingen.

König ist der Hirtenknabe,
Grüner Hügel ist sein Thron,
Über seinem Haupt die Sonne
Ist die schwere, goldne Kron.

Ihm zu Füßen liegen Schafe,
Weiche Schmeichler, rotbekreuzt;
Kavaliere sind die Kälber,
Und sie wandeln stolz gespreizt.

many a fine thing of him, and on this morning he let me see his Harz, as it is not, most assuredly, seen by every one. But the Harz also saw me as I am seen by few, and there were as costly pearls on my eyelashes, as on the grass of the valley. The morning dew of love wetted my cheeks, the rustling pines understood me, their parting twigs waved up and down, as if, like mute mortals, they would express their joy with gestures of their hands, and from afar, I heard beautiful and mysterious chimes, like the bell tones of some long-lost forest church. People say that these sounds are caused by the cattle bells, which in the Harz ring with remarkable clearness and purity.

It was noon, according to the position of the sun, as I chanced upon such a flock; and its herd, a friendly, lighthaired young fellow, told me that the great hill at whose base I stood, was the old world-renowned Brocken. For many leagues around there is no house, and I was glad enough when the young man invited me to share his meal. We sat down to a déjeuner dinatoire, consisting of bread and cheese. The sheep snatched up our crumbs, while pretty shining heifers jumped around, ringing their bells roguishly, and laughing at us with great merry eyes. We made a royal meal, my host appearing to me altogether a king; and as he is the only monarch who has ever given me bread,[59] I will sing him right royally.

The shepherd is a monarch,[60]
A hillock is his throne,
The sun above him shining,
Is his heavy golden crown.

Sheep at his feet are lying,
Soft flatterers, crossed with red,
The calves are cavalieros,
Who strut with haughty head.

Hofschauspieler sind die Böcklein,
Und die Vögel und die Küh,
Mit den Flöten, mit den Glöcklein,
Sind die Kammermusici.

Und das klingt und singt so lieblich,
Und so lieblich rauschen drein
Wasserfall und Tannenbäume,
Und der König schlummert ein.

Unterdessen muß regieren
Der Minister, jener Hund,
Dessen knurriges Gebelle
Widerhallet in der Rund.

Schläfrig lallt der junge König:
»Das Regieren ist so schwer,
Ach, ich wollt, daß ich zu Hause
Schon bei meiner Köngin wär!

In den Armen meiner Köngin
Ruht mein Königshaupt so weich,
Und in ihren lieben Augen
Liegt mein unermeßlich Reich!«

Wir nahmen freundschaftlich Abschied, und fröhlich stieg
ich den Berg hinauf. Bald empfing mich eine Waldung himmel-
hoher Tannen, für die ich, in jeder Hinsicht, Respekt habe.
Diesen Bäumen ist nämlich das Wachsen nicht so ganz leicht
gemacht worden, und sie haben es sich in der Jugend sauer
werden lassen. Der Berg ist hier mit vielen großen Granit-
blöcken übersäet, und die meisten Bäume mußten mit ihren
Wurzeln diese Steine umranken oder sprengen, und mühsam
den Boden suchen, woraus sie Nahrung schöpfen können. Hier
und da liegen die Steine, gleichsam ein Tor bildend, über einander, und oben darauf stehen die Bäume, die nackten Wurzeln
über jene Steinpforte hinziehend, und erst am Fuße derselben
den Boden erfassend, so daß sie in der freien Luft zu wachsen
scheinen. Und doch haben sie sich zu jener gewaltigen Höhe

Court players are the he goats,
And the wild bird and the cow,
With their piping and their herd bell,
Are the king's musicians now.

They ring and sing so sweetly,
And so sweetly chime around,
The waterfall and fir-trees,
While the monarch slumbers sound.

And as he sleeps, his sheep-dog,
As minister must reign;
His snarling and his barking,
Reecho o'er the plain.

Dozing, the monarch murmurs
"Such work was never seen
As reigning—I were happier
At home beside my queen!

My royal head when weary,
In my queen's arms softly lies,
And my endless broad dominion,
In her deep and gentle eyes."

We took leave of each other in a friendly manner, and with a
light heart I began to ascend the mountain. I was soon welcomed
by a grove of stately firs, for whom I, in every respect, entertain
the most reverential regard. For these trees, of which I speak,
have not found growing to be such an easy business, and during
the days of their youth it fared hard with them. The mountain is
here sprinkled with a great number of blocks of granite, and most
of the trees are obliged either to twine their roots over the stones,
or split them in two, that they may thus with trouble get at a little
earth to nourish them. Here and there stones lie, on each other,
forming as it were a gate, and over all grow the trees, their naked
roots twining down over the wild portals, and first reaching the

empor geschwungen, und mit den umklammerten Steinen wie zusammengewachsen, stehen sie fester als ihre bequemen Kollegen im zahmen Forstboden des flachen Landes. So stehen auch im Leben jene großen Männer, die durch das Überwinden früher Hemmungen und Hindernisse sich erst recht gestärkt und befestigt haben. Auf den Zweigen der Tannen kletterten Eichhörnchen, und unter denselben spazierten die gelben Hirsche. Wenn ich solch ein liebes, edles Tier sehe, so kann ich nicht begreifen, wie gebildete Leute Vergnügen daran finden, es zu hetzen und zu töten. Solch ein Tier war barmherziger als die Menschen, und säugte den schmachtenden Schmerzenreich der heiligen Genoveva.

Allerliebst schossen die goldenen Sonnenlichter durch das dichte Tannengrün. Eine natürliche Treppe bildeten die Baumwurzeln. Überall schwellende Moosbänke; denn die Steine sind fußhoch von den schönsten Moosarten, wie mit hellgrünen Sammetpolstern, bewachsen. Liebliche Kühle und träumerisches Quellengemurmel. Hier und da sieht man, wie das Wasser unter den Steinen silberhell hinrieselt und die nackten Baumwurzeln und Fasern bespült. Wenn man sich nach diesem Treiben hinab beugt, so belauscht man gleichsam die geheime Bildungsgeschichte der Pflanzen und das ruhige Herzklopfen des Berges. An manchen Orten sprudelt das Wasser aus den Steinen und Wurzeln stärker hervor und bildet kleine Kaskaden. Da läßt sich gut sitzen. Es murmelt und rauscht so wunderbar, die Vögel singen abgebrochene Sehnsuchtslaute, die Bäume flüstern wie mit tausend Mädchenzungen, wie mit tausend Mädchenaugen schauen uns an die seltsamen Bergblumen, sie strecken nach uns aus die wundersam breiten, drollig gezackten Blätter, spielend flimmern hin und her die lustigen Sonnenstrahlen, die sinnigen Kräutlein erzählen sich grüne Märchen, es ist alles wie verzaubert, es wird immer heimlicher und heimlicher, ein uralter Traum wird lebendig, die Geliebte erscheint – ach, daß sie so schnell wieder verschwindet!

ground at its base, so that they appear to be growing in the air. And yet they have forced their way up to that startling height, and grown into one with the rocks they stand more securely than their easy comrades, who are rooted in the tame forest soil of the level country. So it is in life with those great men who have strengthened and established themselves by resolutely subduing the obstacles which oppressed their youth. Squirrels climbed amid the fir twigs, while beneath, yellow-brown deer were quietly grazing. I cannot comprehend, when I see such a noble animal, how educated and refined people can take pleasure in its chase or death. Such a creature was once more merciful than man, and suckled the longing Schmerzenreich of the Holy Genoveva.[61]

Most beautiful were the golden sun-rays shooting through the dark green of the firs. The roots of the trees formed a natural stairway, and everywhere my feet encountered swelling beds of moss, for the stones are here covered foot-deep, as if with light-green velvet cushions. Everywhere a pleasant freshness and the dreamy murmur of streams. Here and there we see water rippling silver-clear amid the rocks, washing the bare roots and fibers of trees. Bend down to the current and listen, and you may hear at the same time the mysterious history of the growth of the plants, and the quiet pulsations of the heart of the mountain. In many places the water jets strongly up, amid rocks and roots, forming little cascades. It is pleasant to sit in such places. All murmurs and rustles so sweetly and strangely, the birds carol broken strains of love-longing, the trees whisper like a thousand girls, odd flowers peep up like a thousand maidens' eyes, stretching out to us their curious, broad, droll-pointed leaves, the sun-rays flash here and there in sport, the soft-souled herds are telling their green legends, all seems enchanted, and becomes more secret and confidential, an old, old dream is realized, the loved one appears—alas that all so quickly vanishes!

Je höher man den Berg hinauf steigt, desto kürzer, zwerg-
hafter werden die Tannen, sie scheinen immer mehr und mehr
zusammen zu schrumpfen, bis nur Heidelbeer- und Rotbeer-
sträuche und Bergkräuter übrig bleiben. Da wird es auch schon
fühlbar kälter. Die wunderlichen Gruppen der Granitblöcke,
werden hier erst recht sichtbar; diese sind oft von erstaunlicher
Größe. Das mögen wohl die Spielbälle sein, die sich die bösen
Geister einander zuwerfen in der Walpurgisnacht, wenn hier
die Hexen auf Besenstielen und Mistgabeln einhergeritten
kommen, und die abenteuerlich verruchte Lust beginnt, wie
die glaubhafte Amme es erzählt, und wie es zu schauen ist auf
den hübschen Faustbildern des Meister Retzsch. Ja, ein junger
Dichter, der auf einer Reise von Berlin nach Göttingen in der
ersten Mainacht am Brocken vorbei ritt, bemerkte sogar, wie
einige belletristische Damen auf einer Bergecke ihre ästhetische
Teegesellschaft hielten, sich gemütlich die »Abendzeitung« vor-
lasen, ihre poetischen Ziegenböckchen, die meckernd den Tee-
tisch umhüpften, als Universalgenies priesen und über alle
Erscheinungen in der deutschen Literatur ihr Endurteil fällten;
doch, als sie auch auf den »Ratcliff« und »Almansor« gerieten,
und dem Verfasser alle Frömmigkeit und Christlichkeit ab-
sprachen, da sträubte sich das Haar des jungen Mannes, Entsetzen ergriff ihn – ich gab dem Pferde die Sporen und jagte
vorüber.

In der Tat, wenn man die obere Hälfte des Brockens besteigt,
kann man sich nicht erwehren, an die ergötzlichen Blocksbergs-
geschichten zu denken, und besonders an die große, mystische,
deutsche Nationaltragödie vom Doktor Faust. Mir war immer,
als ob der Pferdefuß neben mir hinauf klettere, und jemand
humoristisch Atem schöpfe. Und ich glaube, auch Mephisto
muß mit Mühe Atem holen, wenn er seinen Lieblingsberg er-
steigt; es ist ein äußerst erschöpfender Weg, und ich war froh,
als ich endlich das langersehnte Brockenhaus zu Gesicht bekam.

Dieses Haus, das, wie durch vielfache Abbildungen bekannt

The higher we ascend, so much the shorter and more dwarf-like do the fir-trees become, shrinking up as it were within themselves, until finally only whortleberries, bilberries, and mountain herbs remain. It is also sensibly colder. Here, for the first time, the granite boulders, which are frequently of enormous size, become fully visible. These may well have been the play-balls which evil spirits[62] cast at each other on the Walpurgis night, when the witches came riding hither on brooms and pitchforks, when the mad, unhallowed revelry begins, as our believing nurses have told us, and as we may see it represented in the beautiful Faust-pictures of Master Retsch.[63] Yes, a young poet who in journeying from Berlin to Göttingen, on the first evening in May, passed the Brocken, remarked how certain belles-lettered ladies held their esthetic tea circle in a rocky corner, how they comfortably read the evening journal, how they praised as an universal genius their pet billy-goat, who, bleating, hopped around their table, and how they passed a final judgment on all the manifestations of German literature. But when they at last fell upon *Ratcliff* and *Almansor,*[64] utterly denying to the author aught like piety or Christianity, the hair of the youth rose on end, terror seized him—I spurred my steed and rode onwards![65]

In fact, when we ascend the upper half of the Brocken, no one can well help thinking of the attractive legends of the Blocksberg, and especially of the great mystical German national tragedy of Doctor Faust. It ever seemed to me that I could hear the cloven foot scrambling along behind, and that some one inhaled an atmosphere of humor. And I verily believe that Mephisto himself must breathe with difficulty when he climbs his favorite mountain, for it is a road which is to the last degree exhausting, and I was glad enough when I at last beheld the long-desired Brocken-house.

This house, as every one knows from numerous pictures, consists

ist, bloß aus einem Rez-de-Chaussee besteht und auf der Spitze des Berges liegt, wurde erst 1800 vom Grafen Stolberg-Wernigerode erbaut, für dessen Rechnung es auch, als Wirtshaus, verwaltet wird. Die Mauern sind erstaunlich dick, wegen des Windes und der Kälte im Winter; das Dach ist niedrig, in der Mitte desselben steht eine turmartige Warte, und bei dem Hause liegen noch zwei kleine Nebengebäude, wovon das eine, in frühern Zeiten, den Brockenbesuchern zum Obdach diente. Der Eintritt in das Brockenhaus erregte bei mir eine etwas ungewöhnliche, märchenhafte Empfindung. Man ist nach einem langen, einsamen Umhersteigen durch Tannen und Klippen plötzlich in ein Wolkenhaus versetzt; Städte, Berge und Wälder blieben unten liegen, und oben findet man eine wunderlich zusammengesetzte, fremde Gesellschaft, von welcher man, wie es an dergleichen Orten natürlich ist, fast wie ein erwarteter Genosse, halb neugierig und halb gleichgültig, empfangen wird. Ich fand das Haus voller Gäste, und wie es einem klugen Manne geziemt, dachte ich schon an die Nacht, an die Unbehaglichkeit eines Strohlagers; mit hinsterbender Stimme verlangte ich gleich Tee, und der Herr Brockenwirt war vernünftig genug, einzusehen, daß ich kranker Mensch für die Nacht ein ordentliches Bett haben müsse. Dieses verschaffte er mir in einem engen Zimmerchen, wo schon ein junger Kaufmann, ein langes Brechpulver in einem braunen Oberrock, sich etabliert hatte.

In der Wirtsstube fand ich lauter Leben und Bewegung. Studenten von verschiedenen Universitäten. Die einen sind kurz vorher angekommen und restaurieren sich, andere bereiten sich zum Abmarsch, schnüren ihre Ranzen, schreiben ihre Namen ins Gedächtnisbuch, erhalten Brockensträuße von den Hausmädchen: da wird in die Wangen gekniffen, gesungen, gesprungen, gejohlt, man fragt, man antwortet, gut Wetter, Fußweg, Prosit, Adieu. Einige der Abgehenden sind auch etwas angesoffen, und diese haben von der schönen Aussicht einen

of a single story, and was erected in the year 1800 by Count Stolberg Wernigerode, for whose profit it is managed as a tavern. On account of the wind and cold in winter, its walls are incredibly thick. The roof is low. From its midst rises a tower-like observatory, and near the house lie two little out-buildings, one of which, in earlier times, served as shelter to the Brocken visitors.

On entering the Brocken-house, I experienced a somewhat unusual and legend-like sensation. After a long, solitary journey, amid rocks and pines, the traveler suddenly finds himself in a house amid the clouds. Far below lie cities, hills and forests, while above he encounters a curiously blended circle of strangers, by whom he is received as is usual in such assemblies, almost like an expected companion—half inquisitively and half indifferently. I found the house full of guests, and, as becomes a wise man, I first reflected on the night, and the discomfort of sleeping on straw. My part was at once determined on. With the voice of one dying I called for tea, and the Brocken landlord was reasonable enough to perceive that the sick gentleman must be provided with a decent bed. This he gave me, in a narrow room, where a young merchant—a long emetic in a brown overcoat— had already established himself.

In the public room I found a full tide of bustle and animation. There were students from different universities. Some of the newly arrived were taking refreshments. Others, preparing for departure, buckled on their knapsacks, wrote their names in the album, and received bouquets from the housemaid. There was jesting, singing, springing, trilling, some questioning, some answering, fine weather, foot-path, prosit!—luck be with you! Adieu! Some of those leaving were also partly drunk, and these derived a twofold pleasure from the beautiful scenery, for a tipsy man sees double.

doppelten Genuß, da ein Betrunkener alles doppelt sieht.
Nachdem ich mich ziemlich rekreiert, bestieg ich die Turm-
warte, und fand daselbst einen kleinen Herrn mit zwei Damen,
einer jungen und einer ältlichen. Die junge Dame war sehr
schön. Eine herrliche Gestalt, auf dem lockigen Haupte ein
helmartiger, schwarzer Atlashut, mit dessen weißen Federn die
Winde spielten, die schlanken Glieder von einem schwarz-
seidenen Mantel so fest umschlossen, daß die edlen Formen
hervortraten, und das freie, große Auge ruhig hinabschauend
in die freie, große Welt.

Als ich noch ein Knabe war, dachte ich an nichts als an
Zauber- und Wundergeschichten, und jede schöne Dame, die
Straußfedern auf dem Kopfe trug, hielt ich für eine Elfenköni-
gin, und bemerkte ich gar, daß die Schleppe ihres Kleides naß
war, so hielt ich sie für eine Wassernixe. Jetzt denke ich anders,
seit ich aus der Naturgeschichte weiß, daß jene symbolischen
Federn von dem dümmsten Vogel herkommen, und daß die
Schleppe eines Damenkleides auf sehr natürliche Weise naß
werden kann. Hätte ich mit jenen Knabenaugen die erwähnte
junge Schöne, in erwähnter Stellung, auf dem Brocken gesehen, so würde ich sicher gedacht haben: das ist die Fee des
Berges, und sie hat eben den Zauber ausgesprochen, wodurch
dort unten alles so wunderbar erscheint. Ja, in hohem·Grade
wunderbar erscheint uns alles beim ersten Hinabschauen vom
Brocken, alle Seiten unseres Geistes empfangen neue Ein-
drücke, und diese, meistens verschiedenartig, sogar sich wider-
sprechend, verbinden sich in unserer Seele zu einem großen,
noch unentworrenen, unverstandenen Gefühl. Gelingt es uns,
dieses Gefühl in seinem Begriffe zu erfassen, so erkennen wir
den Charakter des Berges. Dieser Charakter ist ganz deutsch,
sowohl in Hinsicht seiner Fehler, als auch seiner Vorzüge. Der
Brocken ist ein Deutscher. Mit deutscher Gründlichkeit zeigt
er uns, klar und deutlich, wie ein Riesenpanorama, die vielen
hundert Städte, Städtchen und Dörfer, die meistens nördlich

After recruiting myself, I ascended the observatory, and there found a little gentleman, with two ladies, one of whom was young and the other elderly. The young lady was very beautiful. A superb figure, flowing locks, surmounted by a helm-like black satin chapeau, amid whose white plumes the wind played; fine limbs, so closely enwrappcd by a black silk mantle that their exquisite form was made manifest, and great free eyes, calmly looking down into the great free world.

When as yet a boy I thought of naught save tales of magic and wonder, and every fair lady who had ostrich feathers on her head I regarded as an elfin queen. If I observed that the train of her dress was wet, I believed at once that she must be a water fairy. Now I know better, having learned from Natural History that those symbolical feathers are found on the most stupid of birds, and that the skirt of a lady's dress may be wetted in a very natural way. But if I had, with those boyish eyes, seen the aforesaid young lady, in the aforesaid position on the Brocken, I would most assuredly have thought, "That is the fairy of the mountain and she has just uttered the charm which has caused all down there to appear so wonderful." Yes, at the first glance from the Brocken, everything appears in a high degree marvelous—new impressions throng in on every side, and these, varied and often contradictory, unite in our soul to an overpowering and confusing sensation. If we succeed in grasping the idea of this sensation, we shall comprehend the character of the mountain. This character is entirely German as regards not only its advantages, but also its defects. The Brocken is a German. With German thoroughness he points out to us— sharply and accurately defined as in a panorama—the hundreds of cities, towns, and villages which are principally situated to the north, and all the mountains, forests, rivers, and plains which lie infinitely far around. But for this very cause everything

liegen, und ringsum alle Berge, Wälder, Flüsse, Flächen, unendlich weit. Aber eben dadurch erscheint alles wie eine scharf gezeichnete, rein illuminierte Spezialkarte, nirgends wird das Auge durch eigentlich schöne Landschaften erfreut; wie es denn immer geschieht, daß wir deutschen Kompilatoren wegen der ehrlichen Genauigkeit, womit wir alles und alles hingeben wollen, nie daran denken können, das einzelne auf eine schöne Weise zu geben. Der Berg hat auch so etwas Deutsch-ruhiges, Verständiges, Tolerantes; eben weil er die Dinge so weit und klar überschauen kann. Und wenn solch ein Berg seine Riesenaugen öffnet, mag er wohl noch etwas mehr sehen, als wir Zwerge, die wir mit unsern blöden Äuglein auf ihm herum klettern. Viele wollen zwar behaupten, der Brocken sei sehr philiströse, und Claudius sang: »Der Blocksberg ist der lange Herr Philister!« Aber das ist Irrtum. Durch seinen Kahlkopf, den er zuweilen mit einer weißen Nebelkappe bedeckt, gibt er sich zwar einen Anstrich von Philiströsität; aber, wie bei manchen andern großen Deutschen, geschieht es aus purer Ironie. Es ist sogar notorisch, daß der Brocken seine burschikosen, phantastischen Zeiten hat, z.B. die erste Mainacht. Dann wirft er seine Nebelkappe jubelnd in die Lüfte, und wird, eben so gut wie wir übrigen, recht echtdeutsch romantisch verrückt.

Ich suchte gleich die schöne Dame in ein Gespräch zu verflechten: denn Naturschönheiten genießt man erst recht, wenn man sich auf der Stelle darüber aussprechen kann. Sie war nicht geistreich, aber aufmerksam sinnig. Wahrhaft vornehme Formen. Ich meine nicht die gewöhnliche, steife, negative Vornehmheit, die genau weiß, was unterlassen werden muß; sondern jene seltnere, freie, positive Vornehmheit, die uns genau sagt, was wir tun dürfen, und die uns, bei aller Unbefangenheit, die höchste gesellige Sicherheit gibt. Ich entwickelte, zu meiner eigenen Verwunderung, viele geographische Kenntnisse, nannte der wißbegierigen Schönen alle Namen der Städte, die vor uns lagen, suchte und zeigte ihr dieselben auf meiner

appears like an accurately designed and perfectly colored map, and nowhere is the eye gratified by really beautiful landscapes— just as we German compilers, owing to the honorable exactness with which we attempt to give all and everything, never appear to think of giving integral parts in a beautiful manner. The mountain in consequence has a certain calm-German, intelligent, tolerant character, simply because he can see things so distant, yet so distinctly. And when such a mountain opens his giant eyes, it may be that he sees somewhat more than we dwarfs, who with our weak eyes climb over him. Many, indeed, assert that the Blocksberg is very Philistine-like, and Claudius once sang "The Blocksberg is the lengthy Sir Philistine."[66] But that was an error. On account of his bald head, which he occasionally covers with a cloud cap, the Blocksberg has indeed something of a Philistine-like aspect, but this with him, as with many other great Germans, is the result of pure irony. For it is notorious that he has his wild-student and fantastic times, as for instance on the first night of May. Then he casts his cloud cap uproariously and merrily on high, and becomes like the rest of us, real German romantic mad.

I soon sought to entrap the beauty into a conversation, for we only begin to fully enjoy the beauties of nature when we talk about them on the spot. She was not spirituelle, but attentively intelligent. Both were perfect models of gentility. I do not mean that commonplace, stiff, negative respectability, which knows exactly what must not be done or said, but that rarer, independent positive gentility, which inspires an accurate knowledge of what we may venture on, and which amid all our ease and abandon inspires the utmost social confidence. I developed to my own amazement much geographical knowledge, detailed to the curious beauty the names of all the towns which lay before us, and sought them out for her on the map, which with all the

Landkarte, die ich über den Steintisch, der in der Mitte der Turmplatte steht, mit echter Dozentenmiene ausbreitete. Manche Stadt konnte ich nicht finden, vielleicht weil ich mehr mit den Fingern suchte, als mit den Augen, die sich unterdessen auf dem Gesicht der holden Dame orientierten, und dort schönere Partien fanden, als »Schierke« und »Elend«. Dieses Gesicht gehörte zu denen, die nie reizen, selten entzücken, und immer gefallen. Ich liebe solche Gesichter, weil sie mein schlimmbewegtes Herz zur Ruhe lächeln.

In welchem Verhältnis der kleine Herr, der die Damen begleitete, zu denselben stehen mochte, konnte ich nicht erraten. Es war eine dünne, merkwürdige Figur. Ein Köpfchen, sparsam bedeckt mit grauen Härchen, die über die kurze Stirn bis an die grünlichen Libellenaugen reichten, die runde Nase weit hervor tretend, dagegen Mund und Kinn sich wieder ängstlich nach den Ohren zurück ziehend. Dieses Gesichtchen schien aus einem zarten, gelblichen Tone zu bestehen, woraus die Bildhauer ihre ersten Modelle kneten; und wenn die schmalen Lippen zusammen kniffen, zogen sich über die Wangen einige tausend halbkreisartige, feine Fältchen. Der kleine Mann sprach kein Wort, und nur dann und wann, wenn die ältere Dame ihm etwas Freundliches zuflüsterte, lächelte er wie ein Mops, der den Schnupfen hat.

Jene ältere Dame war die Mutter der jüngeren, und auch sie besaß die vornehmsten Formen. Ihr Auge verriet einen krankhaft schwärmerischen Tiefsinn, um ihren Mund lag strenge Frömmigkeit, doch schien mirs, als ob er einst sehr schön gewesen sei, und viel gelacht und viele Küsse empfangen und viele erwidert habe. Ihr Gesicht glich einem Codex palimpsestus, wo, unter der neuschwarzen Mönchsschrift eines Kirchenvatertextes, die halberloschenen Verse eines altgriechischen Liebesdichters hervorlauschen. Beide Damen waren mit ihrem Begleiter dieses Jahr in Italien gewesen, und erzählten mir allerei Schönes von Rom, Florenz und Venedig. Die Mutter erzählte

solemnity of a teacher I had spread out on the stone table which stands in the center of the tower. I could not find many of the towns, possibly because I sought them more with my fingers than with my eyes, which latter were scanning the face of the fair lady, and discovering in it fairer regions than those of Schierke and Elend.[67] This countenance was one of those which never excite, and seldom enrapture, but which always please. I love such faces, for they smile my evilly agitated heart to rest.

I could not divine the relation in which the little gentleman stood to the ladies whom he accompanied. He was a spare and remarkable figure, A head sprinkled with gray hair, which fell over his low forehead down to his dragon-fly eyes, and a round, broad nose which projected boldly forwards, while his mouth and chin seemed retreating in terror back to his ears. His face looked as if formed of the soft yellowish clay with which sculptors mold their first models, and when the thin lips pinched together, thousands of semicircular and faint wrinkles appeared on his cheeks. The little man never spoke a word, only at times when the elder lady whispered something friendly in his ear, he smiled like a lap-dog which has taken cold.

The elder lady was the mother of the younger, and she too was gifted with an air of extreme respectability and refinement. Her eyes betrayed a sickly, dreamy depth of thought, and about her mouth there was an expression of confirmed piety, yet withal it seemed to me that she had once been very beautiful, and often smiled, and taken and given many a kiss. Her countenance resembled a codex palimpsestus, in which, from beneath the recent black monkish writing of some text of a Church Father, there peeped out the half obliterated verse of an old Greek love poet. Both ladies had been that year with their companion in Italy, and told me many things of the beauties of Rome, Florence, and Venice. The mother had much to say of the pictures of

viel von den Raphaelschen Bildern in der Peterskirche; die
Tochter sprach mehr von der Oper im Theater Fenice.

Derweilen wir sprachen, begann es zu dämmern: die Luft
wurde noch kälter, die Sonne neigte sich tiefer, und die Turmplatte füllte sich mit Studenten, Handwerksburschen und
einigen ehrsamen Bürgerleuten samt deren Ehefrauen und
Töchtern, die alle den Sonnenuntergang sehen wollten. Es ist
ein erhabener Anblick, der die Seele zum Gebet stimmt. Wohl
eine Viertelstunde standen alle ernsthaft schweigend, und sahen,
wie der schöne Feuerball im Westen allmählig versank; die
Gesichter wurden vom Abendrot angestrahlt, die Hände falte-
ten sich unwillkürlich; es war, als ständen wir, eine stille Gemeinde, im Schiffe eines Riesendoms, und der Priester erhöbe
jetzt den Leib des Herrn, und von der Orgel herab ergösse sich
Palestrinas ewiger Choral.

Während ich so in Andacht versunken stehe, höre ich, daß
neben mir jemand ausruft: »Wie ist die Natur doch im allgemeinen so schön!« Diese Worte kamen aus der gefühlvollen
Brust meines Zimmergenossen, des jungen Kaufmanns. Ich
gelangte dadurch wieder zu meiner Werkeltagsstimmung, war
jetzt im Stande, den Damen über den Sonnenuntergang recht
viel Artiges zu sagen, und sie ruhig, als wäre nichts passiert,
nach ihrem Zimmer zu führen. Sie erlaubten mir auch, sie noch
eine Stunde zu unterhalten. Wie die Erde selbst drehte sich
unsre Unterhaltung um die Sonne. Die Mutter äußerte: die in
Nebel versinkende Sonne habe ausgesehen wie eine glühende
Rose, die der galante Himmel herab geworfen in den weit
ausgebreiteten, weißen Brautschleier seiner geliebten Erde. Die
Tochter lächelte und meinte, der öftere Anblick solcher Natur-
erscheinungen schwäche ihren Eindruck. Die Mutter berichtigte
diese falsche Meinung durch eine Stelle aus Goethes Reise-
briefen, und frug mich, ob ich den Werther gelesen? Ich
glaube, wir sprachen auch von Angorakatzen, etruskischen
Vasen, türkischen Shawls, Makkaroni und Lord Byron, aus

Raphael in St. Peter's; the daughter spoke more of the opera in La Fenice.

While we conversed, the sun sank lower and lower, the air grew colder, twilight stole over us, and the tower plat form was filled with students, traveling mechanics, and a few honest citizens with their spouses and daughters, all of whom were desirous of witnessing the sunset. That is truly a sublime spectacle, which elevates the soul to prayer. For a full quarter of an hour all stood in solemn silence, gazing on the beautiful fire-ball as it sank in the west; faces were rosy in the evening red; hands were involuntarily folded; it seemed as if we, a silent congregation, stood in the nave of a giant church, that the priest raised the body of the Lord, and that Palestrina's everlasting choral song poured forth from the organ.

As I stood thus lost in piety, I heard some one near me exclaim, "Ah! how beautiful Nature is, as a general thing!" These words came from the full heart of my roommate, the young shopman. This brought me back to my week-day state of mind, and I found myself in tune to say a few neat things to the ladies about the sunset, and to accompany them, as calmly as if nothing had happened, to their room. They permitted me to converse an hour longer with them. Our conversation, like the earth's course, was about the sun. The mother declared that the sun as it sank in the snowy clouds seemed like a red glowing rose, which the gallant heaven had thrown upon the white and spreading bridal veil of his loved earth. The daughter smiled, and thought that a frequent observation of such phenomena weakened their impression. The mother corrected this error by a quotation from Goethe's *Letters of Travel*,[68] and asked me if I had read *Werther*.[69] I believe that we also spoke of Angora cats, Etruscan vases, Turkish shawls, macaroni, and Lord Byron, from whose poems the elder lady, while daintily lisping and sighing, recited several sunset quotations. To

dessen Gedichten die ältere Dame einige Sonnenuntergangs-
stellen, recht hübsch lispelnd und seufzend, rezitierte. Der
jüngern Dame, die kein Englisch verstand, und jene Gedichte
kennen lernen wollte, empfahl ich die Übersetzungen meiner
schönen, geistreichen Landsmännin, der Baronin Elise von
Hohenhausen; bei welcher Gelegenheit ich nicht ermangelte,
wie ich gegen junge Damen zu tun pflege, über Byrons Gott-
losigkeit, Lieblosigkeit, Trostlosigkeit, und der Himmel weiß
was noch mehr, zu eifern.

Nach diesem Geschäfte ging ich noch auf dem Brocken
spazieren; denn ganz dunkel wird es dort nie. Der Nebel war
nicht stark, und ich betrachtete die Umrisse der beiden Hügel,
die man den Hexenaltar und die Teufelskanzel nennt. Ich schoß
meine Pistolen ab, doch es gab kein Echo. Plötzlich aber höre
ich bekannte Stimmen und fühle mich umarmt und geküßt. Es
waren meine Landsleute, die Göttingen vier Tage später verlassen hatten, und bedeutend erstaunt waren, mich ganz allein
auf dem Blocksberge wieder zu finden. Da gab es ein Erzählen
und Verwundern und Verabreden, ein Lachen und Erinnern,
welches freudige Wiedersehen!

Im großen Zimmer wurde eine Abendmahlzeit gehalten.
Ein langer Tisch mit zwei Reihen hungriger Studenten. Im
Anfange gewöhnliches Universitätsgespräch: Duelle, Duelle
und wieder Duelle. Die Gesellschaft bestand meistens aus
Hallensern, und Halle wurde daher Hauptgegenstand der
Unterhaltung. Die Fensterscheiben des Hofrats Schütz wurden
exegetisch beleuchtet. Dann erzählte man, daß die letzte Cour
bei dem König von Cypern sehr glänzend gewesen sei, daß er
einen natürlichen Sohn erwählt, daß er sich eine lichtensteinsche
Prinzessin ans linke Bein antrauen lassen, daß er die Staats-
mätresse abgedankt, und daß das ganze gerührte Ministerium
vorschriftmäßig geweint habe. Ich brauche wohl nicht zu er-
wähnen, daß sich dieses auf Hallesche Bierwürden bezieht.
Hernach kamen die zwei Chinesen aufs Tapet, die sich vor zwei

the younger lady, who did not understand English, and who wished to become familiar with those poems, I recommended the translation of my fair and gifted countrywoman, the Baroness Elise von Hohenhausen.[70] On this occa sion, as is my custom when talking with young ladies, I did not neglect to speak of Byron's impiety, heartlessness, cheerlessness, and heaven knows what beside.[71]

After this business I took a walk on the Brocken, for there it is never quite dark. The mist was not heavy, and I could see the outlines of the two hills, known as the Witch's Altar and the Devil's Pulpit. I fired my pistol, but there was no echo. But suddenly I heard familiar voices, and found myself embraced and kissed. The newcomers were fellow students, from my own part of Germany, and had left Göttingen four days later than I. Great was their astonishment at finding me alone on the Blocksberg. Then came a flood-tide of narrative, of astonishment, and of appointment making—of laughing and of recollection![72]

In the great room we had supper. There was a long table, with two rows of hungry students. At first we had only the usual subject of University conversation—duels, duels, and once again duels. The company consisted principally of Halle students,[73] and Halle formed in consequence the nucleus of their discourse. The window-panes of Court Counselor Schütz[74] were exegetically lighted up. Then it was mentioned that the king of Cyprus's last levee had been very brilliant, that the monarch had appointed a natural son, that he had married—over the left—a princess of the house of Lichtenstein, that the state mistress had been forced to resign, and that the entire ministry, greatly moved, had wept according to rule. I need hardly explain that this all referred to certain beer dignitaries in Halle.[75] Then the two Chinese, who two years before had been exhibited in Berlin, and who were now appointed professors of Chinese esthetics in

Jahren in Berlin sehen ließen, und jetzt in Halle zu Privatdozenten der chinesischen Ästhetik abgerichtet werden. Nun
wurden Witze gerissen. Man setzte den Fall: ein Deutscher
ließe sich in China für Geld sehen; und zu diesem Zwecke
wurde ein Anschlagzettel geschmiedet, worin die Mandarinen
Tsching-Tschang-Tschung und Hi-Ha-Ho begutachteten, daß
es ein echter Deutscher sei, worin ferner seine Kunststücke auf-
gerechnet wurden, die hauptsächlich in Philosophieren, Tabak-
rauchen und Geduld bestanden, und worin noch schließlich bemerkt wurde, daß man um zwölf Uhr, welches die Fütterungs-
stunde sei, keine Hunde mitbringen dürfe, indem diese dem
armen Deutschen die besten Brocken wegzuschnappen pflegten.

Ein junger Burschenschafter, der kürzlich zur Purifikation
in Berlin gewesen, sprach viel von dieser Stadt; aber sehr ein-
seitig. Er hatte Wisotzki und das Theater besucht; beide be-
urteilte er falsch. »Schnell fertig ist die Jugend mit dem Wort
usw.« Er sprach von Garderobeaufwand, Schauspieler- und
Schauspielerinnenskandal usw. Der junge Mensch wußte nicht,
daß, da in Berlin überhaupt der Schein der Dinge am meisten
gilt, was schon die allgemeine Redensart »man so duhn« hin-
länglich andeutet, dieses Scheinwesen auf den Brettern erst recht
florieren muß, und daß daher die Intendanz am meisten zu
sorgen hat für die »Farbe des Barts, womit eine Rolle gespielt
wird«, für die Treue der Kostüme, die von beeidigten Histori-
kern vorgezeichnet und von wissenschaftlich gebildeten
Schneidern genäht werden. Und das ist notwendig. Denn trüge
mal Maria Stuart eine Schürze, die schon zum Zeitalter der
Königin Anna gehört, so würde gewiß der Bankier Christian
Gumpel sich mit Recht beklagen, daß ihm dadurch alle Illusion
verloren gehe; und hätte mal Lord Burleigh aus Versehen die
Hosen von Heinrich IV. angezogen, so würde gewiß die
Kriegsrätin von Steinzopf, geb. Lilientau, diesen Anachronis-
mus den ganzen Abend nicht aus den Augen lassen. Solche
täuschende Sorgfalt der Generalintendanz erstreckt sich aber

Halle, were discussed. Some one supposed a case in which a live German might be exhibited for money in China. Placards would be pasted up, in which. the Mandarins Tsching-Tschang-Tschung and Hi-Ha-Ho certified that the man was a genuine Teuton, including a list of his accomplishments, which consisted principally of philosophizing, smoking, and endless patience. As a finale, visitors might be prohibited from bringing any dogs with them at twelve o'clock (the hour for feeding the captive), as these animals would be sure to snap from the poor German all his titbits.

A young Burschenschafter, who had recently passed his period of purification in Berlin,[76] spoke much, but very partially of this city. He had been constant in his attendance on Wisotzki[77] and the Theater, but judged falsely of both. "For youth is ever ready with a word, etc."[78] He spoke of wardrobe expenditures, theatrical scandal, and similar matters. The youth knew not that in Berlin, where outside show exerts the greatest influence (as is abundantly evidenced by the commonness of the phrase "so people do"), this apparent life must first of all flourish on the stage, and consequently that the especial care of the Direction[79] must be for "the color of the beard with which a part is played," and for the truthfulness of the dresses, which are designed by sworn historians, and sewed by scientifically instructed tailors. And this is indispensable. For if Maria Stuart wore an apron belonging to the time of Queen Anne, the banker, Christian Gumpel,[80] would with justice complain that the anachronism destroyed the illusion, and if Lord Burleigh[81] in a moment of forgetfulness, should don the hose of Henry the Fourth, then Madam, the war counselor Von Steinzopf's wife, *née* Lilienthau, would not get the error out of her head for the whole evening. And this delusive care on the part of the general direction extends itself not only to aprons and pantaloons, but also to the

nicht bloß auf Schürzen und Hosen, sondern auch auf die darin verwickelten Personen. So soll künftig der Othello von einem wirklichen Mohren gespielt werden, den Professor Lichtenstein schon zu diesem Behufe aus Afrika verschrieben hat; in »Menschenhaß und Reue« soll künftig die Eulalia von einem wirklich verlaufenen Weibsbilde, der Peter von einem wirklich dummen Jungen, und der Unbekannte von einem wirklich geheimen Hahnrei gespielt werden, die man alle drei nicht erst aus Afrika zu verschreiben braucht. Hatte nun oben-erwähnter junger Mensch die Verhältnisse des Berliner Schau-spiels schlecht begriffen, so merkte er noch viel weniger, daß die Spontinische Janitscharen-Oper, mit ihren Pauken, Ele-fanten, Trompeten und Tamtams, ein heroisches Mittel ist, um unser erschlafftes Volk kriegerisch zu stärken, ein Mittel, das schon Plato und Cicero staatspfiffig empfohlen haben. Am allerwenigsten begriff der junge Mensch die diplomatische Bedeutung des Balletts. Mit Mühe zeigte ich ihm, wie in Ho-guets Füßen mehr Politik sitzt als in Buchholz' Kopf, wie alle seine Tanztouren diplomatische Verhandlungen bedeuten, wie jede seiner Bewegungen eine politische Beziehung habe, so z.B., daß er unser Kabinett meint, wenn er, sehnsüchtig vor-gebeugt, mit den Händen weit ausgreift; daß er den Bundestag meint, wenn er sich hundertmal auf einem Fuße herumdreht, ohne vom Fleck zu kommen; daß er die kleinen Fürsten im Sinne hat, wenn er wie mit gebundenen Beinen herumtrippelt; daß er das europäische Gleichgewicht bezeichnet, wenn er wie ein Trunkener hin und her schwankt; daß er einen Kongreß andeutet, wenn er die gebogenen Arme knäuelartig in einander verschlingt, und endlich, daß er unsern allzugroßen Freund im Osten darstellt, wenn er in allmähliger Entfaltung sich in die Höhe hebt, in dieser Stellung lange ruht und plötzlich in die erschrecklichsten Sprünge ausbricht. Dem jungen Manne fielen die Schuppen von den Augen, und jetzt merkte er, warum Tänzer besser honoriert werden, als große Dichter, warum das

within enclosed persons. So in future Othello will be played by a real Moor, for whom Professor Lichtenstein[82] has already written to Africa; the "misanthropy and remorse"[83] of Eulalia are to be sustained by a lady who has really wandered from the paths of virtue; Peter will be played by a real blockhead, and the Stranger by a genuine mysterious wittol—for which last three characters it will not be necessary to send to Africa. But little as this young man had comprehended the relations of the Berlin drama, still less was he aware that the Spontini[84] Janizary opera with its kettledrums, elephants, trumpets, and gongs is a heroic means of inspiring with valor our sleeping race—a means once shrewdly recommended by Plato and Cicero. Least of all did the youth comprehend the diplomatic inner meaning of the ballet. It was with great trouble that I finally made him understand that there was really more political science in Hoguet's feet[85] than in Buckholtz's head,[86] that all his *tours de danse* signified diplomatic negotiations, and that his every movement hinted at state matters, as, for instance, when he bent forward anxiously, widely grasping out with his hands, he meant our Cabinet, that a hundred pirouettes on one toe without quitting the spot alluded to the alliance of Deputies, that he was thinking of the lesser princes when he tripped around with his legs tied, that he described the European balance of power when he tottered hither and thither like a drunken man, that he hinted at a Congress when he twisted his bended arms together like a skein, and finally that he sets forth our altogether too great friend in the East, when very gradually unfolding himself he rises on high, stands for a long time in this elevated position, and then all at once breaks out into the most terrifying leaps. The scales fell from the eyes of the young man, and he now saw how it was that dancers are better paid than great poets, why ·the ballet forms in diplomatic circles an inexhaustible subject

Ballett beim diplomatischen Korps ein unerschöpflicher Gegenstand des Gesprächs ist, und warum oft eine schöne Tänzerin noch privatim von dem Minister unterhalten wird, der sich gewiß Tag und Nacht abmüht, sie für sein politisches Systemchen empfänglich zu machen. Beim Apis! wie groß ist die Zahl der exoterischen, und wie klein die Zahl der esoterischen Theaterbesucher! Da steht das blöde Volk und gafft und bewundert Sprünge und Wendungen, und studiert Anatomie in den Stellungen der Lemiere, und applaudiert die Entrechats der Röhnisch, und schwatzt von Grazie, Harmonie und Lenden – und keiner merkt, daß er in getanzten Chiffern das Schicksal des deutschen Vaterlandes vor Augen hat.

Während solcherlei Gespräche hin und her flogen, verlor man doch das Nützliche nicht aus den Augen und den großen Schüsseln, die mit Fleisch, Kartoffeln usw. ehrlich angefüllt waren, wurde fleißig zugesprochen. Jedoch das Essen war schlecht. Dieses erwähnte ich leichthin gegen meinen Nachbar, der aber, mit einem Akzente, woran ich den Schweizer erkannte, gar unhöflich antwortete: daß wir Deutschen wie mit der wahren Freiheit, so auch mit der wahren Genügsamkeit unbekannt seien. Ich zuckte die Achseln und bemerkte: daß die eigentlichen Fürstenknechte und Leckerkramverfertiger überall Schweizer sind und vorzugsweise so genannt werden, und daß überhaupt die jetzigen schweizerischen Freiheitshelden, die so viel Politisch-Kühnes ins Publikum hineinschwatzen, mir immer vorkommen wie Hasen, die auf öffentlichen Jahrmärkten Pistolen abschießen, alle Kinder und Bauern durch ihre Kühnheit in Erstaunen setzen und dennoch Hasen sind.

Der Sohn der Alpen hatte es gewiß nicht böse gemeint, »es war ein dicker Mann, folglich ein guter Mann«, sagt Cervantes. Aber mein Nachbar von der andern Seite, ein Greifswalder, war durch jene Äußerung sehr pikiert; er beteuerte, daß deutsche Tatkraft und Einfältigkeit noch nicht erloschen sei, schlug sich dröhnend auf die Brust und leerte eine ungeheure Stange

of conversation, and why a beautiful danseuse is so frequently privately supported by a minister, who beyond doubt labors night and day that she may obtain a correct idea of his "little system." By Apis! how great is the number of the exoteric, and how small the array of the esoteric frequenters of the theater! There sit the stupid audience, gaping and admiring leaps and attitudes, studying anatomy in the positions of Lemière and applauding the entre-chats of Röhnisch,[87] prattling of "grace," harmony," and "limbs"—no one remarking, meanwhile, that he has before him in choregraphic ciphers the destiny of the German fatherland.

While such observations flitted hither and thither, we did not lose sight of the practical, and the great dishes which were honorably piled up with meat, potatoes, etc., were industriously disposed of. The food, however, was of an indifferent quality. This I carelessly mentioned to my next neighbor at table, who, however, with an accent in which I recognized the Swiss, very impolitely replied, that Germans knew as little of true content as of true liberty. I shrugged my shoulders, remarking, that all the world over the humblest vassals of princes, as well as pastry-cooks and confectioners,[88] were Swiss, and known as a class by that name. I also took the liberty of stating that the Swiss heroes of liberty of the present day reminded me of those tame hares, which we see on market-days in public places, where they fire off pistols to the great amazement of peasants and children—yet remain hares as before.

The son of the Alps had really meant nothing wicked, "he was," as Cervantes says,[89] "a plump man, and consequently a good man." But my neighbor on the other side, a Greifswalder, was deeply touched by the assertion of the Swiss. Energetically did he assert that German ability and simplicity were not as yet extinguished, struck in a threatening manner on his breast, and gulped down a

Weißbier. Der Schweizer sagte: »Nu! Nu!« Doch, je be-
schwichtigender er dieses sagte, desto eifriger ging der Greifswalder ins Geschirr. Dieser war ein Mann aus jenen Zeiten, als
die Läuse gute Tage hatten und die Friseure zu verhungern
fürchteten. Er trug herabhängend langes Haar, ein ritterliches
Barett, einen schwarzen, altdeutschen Rock, ein schmutziges
Hemd, das zugleich das Amt einer Weste versah, und darunter
ein Medaillon mit einem Haarbüschel von Blüchers Schimmel.
Er sah aus wie ein Narr in Lebensgröße. Ich mache mir gern
einige Bewegung beim Abendessen, und ließ mich daher von
ihm in einen patriotischen Streit verflechten. Er war der Meinung, Deutschland müsse in 33 Gauen geteilt werden. Ich
hingegen behauptete: es müßten 48 sein, weil man alsdann ein
systematischeres Handbuch über Deutschland schreiben könne,
und es doch notwendig sei, das Leben mit der Wissenschaft zu
verbinden. Mein Greifswalder Freund war auch ein deutscher
Barde, und wie er mir vertraute, arbeitete er an einem National-
heldengedicht zur Verherrlichung Hermanns und der Her-
mannsschlacht. Manchen nützlichen Wink gab ich ihm für die
Anfertigung dieses Epos. Ich machte ihn darauf aufmerksam,
daß er die Sümpfe und Knüppelwege des Teutoburger Waldes
sehr onomatopöisch durch wäßrige und holprige Verse an-
deuten könne, und daß es eine patriotische Feinheit wäre, wenn
er den Varus und die übrigen Römer lauter Unsinn sprechen
ließe. Ich hoffe, dieser Kunstkniff wird ihm, eben so erfolgreich
wie andern Berliner Dichtern, bis zur bedenklichsten Illusion
gelingen.

An unserem Tische wurde es immer lauter und traulicher, der
Wein verdrängte das Bier, die Punschbowlen dampften, es
wurde getrunken, smolliert und gesungen. Der alte Landes-
vater und herrliche Lieder von W. Müller, Rückert, Uhland
usw. erschollen. Schöne Methfesselsche Melodien. Am aller-
besten erklangen unseres Arndts deutsche Worte: »Der Gott,
der Eisen wachsen ließ, der wollte keine Knechte!« Und drau-

tremendous flagon of white beer. The Swiss said "Nu! nu!" But the more appeasingly and apologetically he said this, so much the faster did the Greifswalder get on with his riot. He was a man of those days when hair-cutters came near dying of starvation. He wore long locks, a knightly cap, a black old German coat, a dirty shirt, which at the same time did duty as a waistcoat, and beneath it a medallion, with a tassel of the hair of Blücher's gray horse.[90] His appearance was that of a full-grown fool. I am always ready for something lively at supper, and consequently held with him a patriotic strife. He was of the opinion that Germany should be divided into thirty-three districts.[91] I asserted on the contrary that there should be forty-eight, because it would then be possible to write a more systematic guide-book for Germany, and because it is essential that life should be blended with science. My Greifswald friend was also a German bard, and, as he informed me in confidence, was occupied with a national heroic poem, in honor of Herrman and the Herrman battle.[92] Many an advantageous hint did I give him on this subject. I suggested to him that the morasses and crooked paths of the Teutobergian forest might be very onomatopoeically indicated by means of watery and ragged verse, and that it would be merely a patriotic liberty should the Romans in his poem chatter the wildest nonsense. I hope that this bit of art will succeed in his works as in those of other Berlin poets, even to the minutest particular.

The company around the table gradually became better acquainted and much noisier. Wine banished beer, punchbowls steamcd, and drinking, smolliren, and singing were the order of the night. The old "Landsfather"[93] and the beautiful songs of W. Müller, Rückert, Uhland,[94] and others rang around, with the exquisite airs of Methfessel.[95] Best of all sounded our own Arndt's German words, "The Lord who bade iron grow, wished for no slaves."[96] And out of doors it roared as if the old mountain

ßen brauste es, als ob der alte Berg mitsänge, und einige schwankende Freunde behaupteten sogar, er schüttle freudig sein kahles Haupt und unser Zimmer werde dadurch hin und her bewegt. Die Flaschen wurden leerer und die Köpfe voller. Der eine brüllte, der andere fistulierte, ein dritter deklamierte aus der »Schuld«, ein vierter sprach Latein, ein fünfter predigte von der Mäßigkeit, und ein sechster stellte sich auf den Stuhl und dozierte: »Meine Herren! Die Erde ist eine runde Walze, die Menschen sind einzelne Stiftchen darauf, scheinbar arglos zerstreut; aber die Walze dreht sich, die Stiftchen stoßen hier und da an und tönen, die einen oft, die andern selten, das gibt eine wunderbare, komplizierte Musik, und diese heißt Weltgeschichte. Wir sprechen also erst von der Musik, dann von der Welt und endsich von der Geschichte; letztere aber teilen wir ein in Positiv und spanische Fliegen – « Und so gings weiter mit Sinn und Unsinn.

Ein gemütlicher Mecklenburger, der seine Nase im Punschglase hatte, und selig lächelnd den Dampf einschnupfte, machte die Bemerkung: es sei ihm zu Mute, als stände er wieder vor dem Theaterbüffet in Schwerin! Ein anderer hielt sein Weinglas wie ein Perspektiv vor die Augen und schien uns aufmerksam damit zu betrachten, während ihm der rote Wein über die Backen ins hervortretende Maul hinablief. Der Greifswalder, plötzlich begeistert, warf sich an meine Brust und jauchzte: »O, verständest Du mich, ich bin ein Liebender, ich bin ein Glücklicher, ich werde wieder geliebt, und, Gott verdamm mich! es ist ein gebildetes Mädchen, denn sie hat volle Brüste, und trägt ein weißes Kleid und spielt Klavier!« – Aber der Schweizer weinte, und küßte zärtlich meine Hand und wimmerte beständig: »O Bäbeli! O Bäbeli!«

In diesem verworrenen Treiben, wo die Teller tanzen und die Gläser fliegen lernten, saßen mir gegenüber zwei Jünglinge, schön und blaß wie Marmorbilder, der eine mehr dem Adonis, der andere mehr dem Apollo ähnlich. Kaum bemerkbar war

sang with us, and a few reeling friends even asserted that he merrily shook his bald head, which caused the great unsteadiness of our floor. The bottles became emptier and the heads of the company fuller. One bellowed like an ox, a second piped, a third declaimed from *The Crime,*[97] a fourth spoke Latin, a fifth preached temperance, and a sixth, assuming the chair learnedly, lectured as follows: "Gentlemen! The world is a round cylinder, upon which human beings, as individual pins, are scattered apparently at random. But the cylinder revolves, the pins knock together and give out tones, some very frequently and others but seldom; all of which causes a remarkably complicated sound, which is generally known as Universal History. We will, in consequence, speak first of music, then of the world, and finally of history; which latter we divide into positive[98] and Spanish flies—" and so sense and nonsense went rattling on.

A jolly Mechlenburger, who held his nose to his punchglass, and, smiling with happiness, snuffed up the perfume, remarked that it caused in him a sensation as if he were standing again before the refreshment table in the Schwerin Theater! Another held his wine-glass like a lorgnette before his eye, and appeared to be carefully studying the company, while the red wine trickled down over his cheek into his projecting mouth. The Greifswalder, suddenly inspired, cast himself upon my breast and shouted wildly, "Oh, that thou couldst understand me, for I am a lover, a happy lover; for I loved again, and G-d d-n me, she's an educated girl, for she has a full bosom, wears a white gown, and plays the piano!" But the Swiss wept, and tenderly kissed my hand, and ever whimpered, "Oh, Molly dear! oh, Molly dear!"[99]

During this crazy scene, in which plates learned to dance and glasses to fly, there sat opposite me two youths, beautiful and pale as statues, one resembling Adonis, the other Apollo. The faint rosy hue which the wine spread over their checks was

der leichte Rosenhauch, den der Wein über ihre Wangen hinwarf. Mit unendlicher Liebe sahen sie sich einander an, als wenn einer lesen könnte in den Augen des andern, und in diesen Augen strahlte es, als wären einige Lichttropfen hinein gefallen aus jener Schale voll lodernder Liebe, die ein frommer Engel dort oben von einem Stern zum andern hinüber trägt. Sie sprachen leise, mit sehnsuchtbebender Stimme, und es waren traurige Geschichten, aus denen ein wunderschmerzlicher Ton hervor klang. »Die Lore ist jetzt auch tot!« sagte der eine und seufzte, und nach einer Pause erzählte er von einem Halleschen Mädchen, das in einen Studenten verliebt war, und als dieser Halle verließ, mit niemand mehr sprach, und wenig aß, und Tag und Nacht weinte, und immer den Kanarienvogel betrachtete, den der Geliebte ihr einst geschenkt hatte. »Der Vogel starb, und bald darauf ist auch die Lore gestorben!« so schloß die Erzählung, und beide Jünglinge schwiegen wieder und seufzten, als wollte ihnen das Herz zerspringen. Endlich sprach der andere: »Meine Seele ist traurig! Komm mit hinaus in die dunkle Nacht! Einatmen will ich den Hauch der Wolken und die Strahlen des Mondes. Genosse meiner Wehmut! ich liebe Dich, Deine Worte tönen wie Rohrgeflüster, wie gleitende Ströme, sie tönen wider in meiner Brust, aber meine Seele ist traurig!«

Nun erhoben sich die beiden Jünglinge, einer schlang den Arm um den Nacken des andern, und sie verließen das tosende Zimmer. Ich folgte ihnen nach und sah, wie sie in eine dunkle Kammer traten, wie der eine, statt des Fensters, einen großen Kleiderschrank öffnete, wie beide vor demselben, mit sehnsüchtig ausgestreckten Armen, stehen blieben und wechselweise sprachen. »Ihr Lüfte der dämmernden Nacht!« rief der erste, »wie erquickend kühlt Ihr meine Wangen! Wie lieblich spielt Ihr mit meinen flatternden Locken! Ich steh auf des Berges wolkigem Gipfel, unter mir liegen die schlafenden Städte der Menschen, und blinken die blauen Gewässer. Horch! dort unten im Tale rauschen die Tannen! Dort über die Hügel zie-

scarcely visible. They gazed on each other with infinite affection, as if the one could read in the eyes of the other, and in those eyes there was a light as though drops of light had fallen therein from the cup of burning love, which an angel on high bears from one star to the other. They conversed softly with earnest, trembling voices, and narrated sad stories, through all of which ran a tone of strange sorrow. "Lore is also dead!" said one, and sighing, proceeded to tell of a maiden of Halle, who had loved a student, and who when the latter left Halle spoke no more to any one, ate but little, wept day and night, gazing ever on the canary-bird which her lover had given her. "The bird died, and Lore did not long survive it," was the conclusion, and both the youths sighed as though their hearts would break. Finally the other said, "My soul is sorrowful[100]—come forth with me into the dark night! Let me inhale the breath of the clouds and the moon-rays. Partake of my sorrows! I love thee, thy words are musical, like the rustling of reeds and the flow of rivulets, they reecho in my breast, but my soul is sorrowful !

Both of the young men arose. One threw his arm around the neck of the other, and thus left the noisy room. I followed, and saw them enter a dark chamber, where the one by mistake, instead of the window, threw open the door of a large wardrobe, and that both, standing before it with outstretched arms, expressing poetic rapture, spoke alternately. "Ye breezes of darkening night," cried the first, "how ye cool and revive my cheeks! How sweetly ye play amid my fluttering locks! I stand on the cloudy peak of the mountain, far below me lie the sleeping cities of men, and blue waters gleam. List! far below in the valley rustle the fir-trees! Far above yonder hills sweep in misty forms the spirits of my fathers. Oh, that I could hunt with ye, on your cloud steeds, through the stormy night, over the rolling sea, upwards to the stars! Alas! I am laden with grief and my soul is

hen, in Nebelgestalten, die Geister der Väter. O, könnt ich mit Euch jagen, auf dem Wolkenroß, durch die stürmische Nacht, über die rollende See, zu den Sternen hinauf! Aber ach! ich bin beladen mit Leid und meine Seele ist traurig!« – Der andere Jüngling hatte ebenfalls seine Arme sehnsuchtsvoll nach dem Kleiderschrank ausgestreckt, Tränen stürzten aus seinen Augen, und zu einer gelbledernen Hose, die er für den Mond hielt, sprach er mit wehmütiger Stimme: »Schön bist du, Tochter des Himmels! Holdselig ist deines Antlitzes Ruhe! Du wandelst einher in Lieblichkeit! Die Sterne folgen deinen blauen Pfaden im Osten. Bei deinem Anblick erfreuen sich die Wolken, und es lichten sich ihre düstern Gestalten. Wer gleicht dir am Himmel, Erzeugte der Nacht? Beschämt in deiner Gegenwart sind die Sterne, und wenden ab die grünfunkelnden Augen. Wohin, wenn des Morgens dein Antlitz erbleicht, entfliehst du von deinem Pfade? Hast du gleich mir deine Halle? Wohnst du im Schatten der Wehmut? Sind deine Schwestern vom Himmel gefallen? Sie, die freudig mit dir die Nacht durchwallten, sind sie nicht mehr? Ja, sie fielen herab, o schönes Licht, und du verbirgst dich oft, sie zu betrauern. Doch einst wird kommen die Nacht, und du, auch du bist vergangen, und hast deine blauen Pfade dort oben verlassen. Dann erheben die Sterne ihre grünen Häupter, die einst deine Gegenwart beschämt, sie werden sich freuen. Doch jetzt bist du gekleidet in deiner Strahlenpracht und schaust herab aus den Toren des Himmels. Zerreißt die Wolken, o Winde, damit die Erzeugte der Nacht hervor zu leuchten vermag, und die buschigen Berge erglänzen und das Meer seine schäumenden Wogen rolle in Licht!«

Ein wohlbekannter, nicht sehr magerer Freund, der mehr getrunken als gegessen hatte, obgleich er auch heute Abend, wie gewöhnlich, eine Portion Rindfleisch verschlungen, wovon sechs Gardeleutnants und ein unschuldiges Kind satt geworden wären, dieser kam jetzt in allzugutem Humor, d. h. ganz en Schwein, vorbeigerannt, schob die beiden elegischen Freunde

sad!" Meanwhile, the other had also stretched out his arms towards the wardrobe, while tears fell from his eyes as he cried to a broad pair of yellow pantaloons which he mistook for the moon. "Fair art thou, Daughter of Heaven![101] Lovely and blessed is the calm of thy countenance. The stars follow thy blue path in the east! At thy glance the clouds rejoice, and their dark brows gleam with light. Who is like unto thee in Heaven, thou the Night-born? The stars are ashamed before thee, and turn away their green sparkling eyes. Whither—ah, whither—when morning pales thy face dost thou flee from thy path? Hast thou, like me, thy hall? Dwellest thou amid shadows of humility? Have thy sisters fallen from Heaven? Are they who joyfully rolled with thee through the night now no more? Yea, they fell adown, O lovely light, and thou hidest thyself to bewail them! Yet the night must at some time come when thou too must pass away, and leave thy blue path above in Heaven. Then the stars, who were once lovely in thy presence, will raise their green heads and rejoice. Now, thou art clothed in thy starry splendor, and gazest adown from the gate of Heaven. Tear aside the clouds, O ye winds, that the night-born may shine forth and the bushy hills gleam, and that the foaming waves of the sea may roll in light!

A well-known and not remarkably thin friend, who had drunk more than he had eaten, though he had already at supper devoured a piece of beef which would have dined six lieutenants of the guard and one innocent child, here came rushing into the room in a very jovial manner, that is to say, *à la* swine, shoved the two elegiac friends one over the other into the wardrobe, stormed through the house door, and began to roar around outside, as if raising the devil in earnest. The noise in the hall grew wilder and louder—the two moaning and weeping friends lay, as they thought, crushed at the foot of the mountain; from their throats ran noble red wine, and the one said to the other,

etwas unsanft in den Schrank hinein, polterte nach der Haustüre, und wirtschaftete draußen ganz mörderisch. Der Lärm im Saal wurde auch immer verworrener und dumpfer. Die beiden Jünglinge im Schranke jammerten und wimmerten, sie lägen zerschmettert am Fuße des Berges; aus dem Hals strömte ihnen der edle Rotwein, sie überschwemmten sich wechselseitig, und der eine sprach zum andern: »Lebe wohl! Ich fühle, daß ich verblute. Warum weckst du mich, Frühlingsluft? Du buhlst und sprichst: ich betaue dich mit Tropfen des Himmels. Doch die Zeit meines Welkens ist nahe, nahe der Sturm, der meine Blätter herabstört! Morgen wird der Wanderer kommen, kommen der mich sah in meiner Schönheit, ringsum wird sein Auge im Felde mich suchen, und wird mich nicht finden. – « Aber alles übertobte die wohlbekannte Baßstimme, die draußen vor der Türe, unter Fluchen und Jauchzen, sich gottlästerlich beklagte: daß auf der ganzen dunkeln Weenderstraße keine einzige Laterne brenne, und man nicht einmal sehen könne, bei wem man die Fensterscheiben eingeschmissen habe.

Ich kann viel vertragen – die Bescheidenheit erlaubt mir nicht, die Bouteillenzahl zu nennen – und ziemlich gut konditioniert gelangte ich nach meinem Schlafzimmer. Der junge Kaufmann lag schon im Bette, mit seiner kreideweißen Nachtmütze und safrangelben Jacke von Gesundheitflanell. Er schlief noch nicht und suchte ein Gespräch mit mir anzuknüpfen. Er war ein Frankfurt-am-Mainer, und folglich sprach er gleich von den Juden, die alles Gefühl für das Schöne und Edle verloren haben, und die englischen Waren 25 Prozent unter dem Fabrikpreise verkaufen. Es ergriff mich die Lust, ihn etwas zu mystifizieren; deshalb sagte ich ihm: ich sei ein Nachtwandler, und müsse im Voraus um Entschuldigung bitten, für den Fall, daß ich ihn etwa im Schlafe stören möchte. Der arme Mensch hat deshalb, wie er mir den andern Tag gestand, die ganze Nacht nicht geschlafen, da er die Besorgnis hegte, ich könnte mit meinen Pistolen, die vor meinem Bette lagen, im Nachtwandler-

"Farewell! I feel that I bleed. Why dost thou waken me,[102] O breath of Spring? Thou caressest me, and sayest, 'I bedew thee with drops from heaven.' But the time of my withering is at hand—at hand the storm which will break away my leaves. To-morrow the Wanderer will come, he who saw me in my beauty—his eyes will glance, as of yore, around the field—in vain—" But over all roared the well-known basso voice without, blasphemously complaining, amid oaths and whoops, that not a single lantern had been lighted along the entire Weender Street, and that one could not even see whose window-panes he had smashed.

I can bear a tolerable quantity—modesty forbids me to say how many bottles—and I consequently retired to my chamber in tolerably good condition. The young merchant already lay in bed, enveloped in his chalk-white nightcap, and yellow Welsh flannel. He was not asleep, and sought to enter into conversation with me. He was a Frankfort-on-Mainer, and consequently spoke at once of the Jews, declared that they had lost all feeling for the beautiful and noble, and that they sold English goods twenty-five per cent under manufacturers' prices. A fancy to humbug him came over me and I told him that I was a somnambulist, and must beforehand beg his pardon should I unwittingly disturb his slumbers. This intelligence, as he confessed the following day, prevented him from sleeping a wink through the whole night, especially since the idea had entered his head that I, while in a somnambulistic crisis, might shoot him with the pistol which lay near my bed. But in truth I fared no better myself, for I slept very little. Dreary and terrifying fancies swept through my brain. A pianoforte extract from Dante's Hell. Finally I dreamed that I saw a law opera, called the "Falcidia,"[103] with libretto on the right of inheritance by Gans,[104] and music by Spontini. A crazy dream! I saw the Roman Forum splendidly

zustande ein Malheur anrichten. Im Grunde war es mir nicht viel besser als ihm gegangen, ich hatte sehr schlecht geschlafen. Wüste, beängstigende Phantasiegebilde. Ein Klavierauszug aus Dantes »Hölle«. Am Ende träumte mir gar, ich sähe die Aufführung einer juristischen Oper, die Falcidia geheißen, erbrechtlicher Text von Gans, und Musik von Spontini. Ein toller Traum. Das römische Forum leuchtete prächtig, Serv. Asinius Göschenus als Prätor auf seinem Stuhle, die Toga in stolze Falten werfend, ergoß sich in polternden Rezitativen; Marcus Tullius Elversus, als Prima Donna legataria, all seine holde Weiblichkeit offenbarend, sang die liebeschmelzende Bravourarie quicunque civis romanus; ziegelrot geschminkte Referendarien brüllten als Chor der Unmündigen; Privatdozenten, als Genien in fleischfarbigen Trikot gekleidet, tanzten ein antejustinianeisches Ballett und bekränzten mit Blumen die zwölf Tafeln, unter Donner und Blitz stieg aus der Erde der beleidigte Geist der römischen Gesetzgebung, hierauf Posaunen, Tamtam Feuerregen, cum omni causa.

Aus diesem Lärmen zog mich der Brockenwirt, indem er mich weckte, um den Sonnenaufgang anzusehen. Auf dem Turm fand ich schon einige Harrende, die sich die frierenden Hände rieben, andere, noch den Schlaf in den Augen, taumelten herauf. Endlich stand die stille Gemeinde von gestern Abend wieder ganz versammelt, und schweigend sahen wir, wie am Horizonte die kleine, karmoisinrote Kugel empor stieg, eine winterlich dämmernde Beleuchtung sich verbreitete, die Berge wie in einem weißwallenden Meere schwammen, und bloß die Spitzen derselben sichtbar hervor traten, so daß man auf einem kleinen Hügel zu stehen glaubte, mitten auf einer überschwemmten Ebene, wo nur hier und da eine trockene Erdscholle hervortritt. Um das Gesehene und Empfundene in Worten festzuhalten, zeichnete ich folgendes Gedicht:

illuminated. In it, Servius Asinius Göschenus[105] sitting as pretor on his chair, and throwing wide his toga in stately folds, burst out into raging recitative; Marcus Tullius Elversus,[106] manifesting as *primadonna legataria* all the exquisite feminineness of his nature, sang the love-melting bravura of *quicunque civis romanus;*[107] referees, rouged red as sealing-wax, bellowed in chorus as minors; private tutors, dressed as genii, in flesh-colored stockinets, danced an ante-Justinian ballet, crowning with flowers the Twelve Tables,[108] while amid thunder and lightning rose from the ground the abused ghost of Roman Legislation, accompanied by trumpets, gongs, fiery rain, *cum omni causa.*

From this confusion I was rescued by the landlord of the Brocken, when he awoke me to see the sunrise. Above, on the tower, I found several already waiting, who rubbed their freezing hands; others, with sleep still in their eyes, stumbled around, until finally the whole silent congregation of the previous evening was reassembled, and we saw how, above the horizon, there rose a little carmine-red ball, spreading a dim, wintry illumination. Far around, amid the mists, rose the mountains, as if swimming in a white rolling sea, only their summits being visible, so that we could imagine ourselves standing on a little hill in the midst of an inundated plain, in which here and there rose dry clods of earth. To retain that which I saw and felt, I sketched the following poem:

Heller wird es schon im Osten
Durch der Sonne kleines Glimmen,
Weit und breit die Bergesgipfel
In dem Nebelmeere schwimmen.

Hätt ich Siebenmeilenstiefel,
Lief ich mit der Hast des Windes
Über jene Bergesgipfel,
Nach dem Haus des lieben Kindes.

Von dem Bettchen, wo sie schlummert,
Zög ich leise die Gardinen,
Leise küßt ich ihre Stirne,
Leise ihres Munds Rubinen.

Und noch leiser wollt ich flüstern
In die kleinen Liljenohren:
Denk im Traum, daß wir uns lieben,
Und daß wir uns nie verloren.

Indessen, meine Sehnsucht nach einem Frühstück war ebenfalls groß, und nachdem ich meinen Damen einige Höflichkeiten gesagt, eilte ich hinab, um in der warmen Stube Kaffee zu trinken. Es tat Not; in meinem Magen sah es so nüchtern aus, wie in der Goslarschen Stephanskirche. Aber mit dem arabischen Trank rieselte mir auch der warme Orient durch die Glieder, östliche Rosen umdufteten mich, süße Bulbul-Lieder erklangen, die Studenten verwandelten sich in Kamele, die Brockenhausmädchen, mit ihren Congrevischen Blicken, wurden zu Houris, die Philisternasen wurden Minarets usw. Das Buch, das neben mir lag, war aber nicht der Koran. Unsinn enthielt es freilich genug. Es war das sogenannte Brockenbuch, worin alle Reisende, die den Berg erstiegen, ihre Namen schreiben, und die meisten noch einige Gedanken, und in Ermangelung derselben, ihre Gefühle hinzu notieren. Viele drükken sich sogar in Versen aus. In diesem Buche sieht man, wel-

In the east 'tis ever brighter,
Though the sun gleams cloudily;
Far and wide the mountain summits
Swim above the misty sea.

Had I seven-mile boots for travel,
Like the fleeting winds I'd rove,
over valley, rock, and river,
To the home of her I love.

From the bed where now she's sleeping
Soft, the curtain I would slip;
Softly kiss her childlike forehead,
Soft the ruby of her lip.

And yet softer would I whisper
In the little snow-white ear:
"Think in dreams that I still love thee,
Think in dreams I'm ever dear."

Meanwhile my desire for breakfast greatly increased, and after paying a few attentions to my ladies, I hastened down to drink coffee in the warm public room. It was full time, for all within me was as sober and as somber as in the St. Stephen's church of Goslar. But with the Arabian beverage, the warm Orient thrilled through my limbs. Eastern roses breathed forth their perfumes on the notes of *bülbül* songs,[110] the students were changed to camels, the Brocken housemaids with their Congreve-rocket[111] glances became houris, the Philistine roses minarets, etc., etc.

But the book which lay near me, though full of nonsense, was not the Koran. It was the so-called Brocken book, in which all travelers who ascend the mountain write their names, many inscribing their thoughts or, in default thereof, their feelings. Many even express themselves in verse. In this book one may

che Greuel entstehen, wenn der große Philistertroß bei gebräuchlichen Gelegenheiten wie hier auf dem Brocken, sich vorgenommen hat, poetisch zu werden. Der Palast des Prinzen von Pallagonia enthält keine so große Abgeschmacktheiten, wie dieses Buch, wo besonders hervor glänzen die Herren Akziseeinnehmer mit ihren verschimmelten Hochgefühlen, die Comptoirjünglinge mit ihren pathetischen Seelenergüssen, die altdeutschen Revolutionsdilettanten mit ihren Turngemeinplätzen, die Berliner Schullehrer mit ihren verunglückten Entzückungsphrasen usw. Herr Johannes Hagel will sich auch mal als Schriftsteller zeigen. Hier wird des Sonnenaufgangs majestätische Pracht beschrieben; dort wird geklagt über schlechtes Wetter, über getäuschte Erwartungen, über den Nebel, der alle Aussicht versperrt. »Benebelt herauf gekommen und benebelt hinunter gegangen!« ist ein stehender Witz, der hier von Hunderten nachgerissen wird.

Das ganze Buch riecht nach Käse, Bier und Tabak; man glaubt einen Roman von Clauren zu lesen.

Während ich nun besagtermaßen Kaffee trank und im Brockenbuche blätterte, trat der Schweizer mit hochroten Wangen herein, und voller Begeisterung erzählte er von dem erhabenen Anblick, den er oben auf dem Turm genossen, als das reine, ruhige Licht der Sonne, Sinnbild der Wahrheit, mit den nächtlichen Nebelmassen gekämpft, daß es ausgesehen habe wie eine Geisterschlacht, wo zürnende Riesen ihre langen Schwerter ausstrecken, geharnischte Ritter, auf bäumenden Rossen, einher jagen, Streitwagen, flatternde Banner, abenteuerliche Tierbildungen aus dem wildesten Gewühle hervor tauchen, bis endlich alles in den wahnsinnigsten Verzerrungen zusammen kräuselt, blasser und blasser zerrinnt, und spurlos verschwindet. Diese demagogische Naturerscheinung hatte ich versäumt, und ich kann, wenn es zur Untersuchung kommt, eidlich versichern: daß ich von nichts weiß, als vom Geschmack des guten braunen Kaffees. Ach, dieser war sogar

observe the horrors which result when the great Philistine Pegasus at convenient opportunities, such as this on the Brocken, becomes poetic. The palace of the Prince of Pallagonia[112] never contained such absurdities and insipidities as are to be found in this book. Those who shine in it, with especial splendor, are Messieurs the excise collectors, with their moldy "high inspirations"; counter jumpers, with their pathetic outgushings of the soul; old German dilettanti with their Turner-union phrases, and Berlin schoolmasters with their unsuccessful efforts at enthusiasm. Mr. Snobbs will also for once show himself as author. In one page, the majestic splendor of the sun is described, in another, complaints occur of bad weather, of disappointed hopes, and of the clouds which obstruct the view. "Went up wet without, and came down wet within," is a standing joke, repeated in the book hundreds of times.

The whole volume smells of beer, tobacco, and cheese, we might fancy it one of Clauren's romances.[113]

While I drank the coffee aforesaid, and turned over the Brocken book, the Swiss entered, his cheeks deeply glowing, and described with enthusiasm the sublime view which he had just enjoyed in the tower above, as the pure calm light of the Sun, that symbol of Truth, fought with the night mists, and that it appeared like a battle of spirits, in which rattling giants brandished their long swords, where harnessed knights on leaping steeds chased each other, and war-chariots, fluttering banners, and extravagant monster forms sank in the wildest confusion, till all finally entwined in the maddest contortions melted into dimness and vanished, leaving no trace. This demagogical natural phenomenon I had neglected, and, should the curious affair be ever made the subject of investigation, I am ready to declare on oath that all I know of the matter is the flavor of the good brown coffee I was then tasting. Alas! this

Schuld, daß ich meine schöne Dame vergessen, und jetzt stand sie vor der Tür, mit Mutter und Begleiter, im Begriff den Wagen zu besteigen. Kaum hatte ich noch Zeit, hin zu eilen und ihr zu versichern, daß es kalt sei. Sie schien unwillig, daß ich nicht früher gekommen; doch ich glättete bald die miß-mütigen Falten ihrer schönen Stirn, indem ich ihr eine wunder-liche Blume schenkte, die ich den Tag vorher, mit halsbrechen-der Gefahr, von einer steilen Felsenwand gepflückt hatte. Die Mutter verlangte den Namen der Blume zu wissen, gleichsam als ob sie es unschicklich fände, daß ihre Tochter eine fremde, unbekannte Blume vor die Brust stecke – denn wirklich, die Blume erhielt diesen beneidenswerten Platz, was sie sich gewiß gestern auf ihrer einsamen Höhe nicht träumen ließ. Der schweigsame Begleiter öffnete jetzt auf einmal den Mund, zählte die Staubfäden der Blume und sagte ganz trocken: »Sie gehört zur achten Klasse.«

Es ärgert mich jedesmal, wenn ich sehe, daß man auch Gottes liebe Blumen, eben so wie uns, in Kasten geteilt hat, und nach ähnlichen Äußerlichkeiten, nämlich nach Staubfäden-Ver-schiedenheit. Soll doch mal eine Einteilung stattfinden, so folge man dem Vorschlage Theophrasts, der die Blumen mehr nach dem Geiste, nämlich nach ihrem Geruch, einteilen wollte. Was mich betrifft, so habe ich in der Naturwissenschaft mein eigenes System, und demnach teile ich alles ein: in dasjenige, was man essen kann, und in dasjenige, was man nicht essen kann.

Jedoch, der ältern Dame war die geheimnisvolle Natur der Blumen nichts weniger als verschlossen, und unwillkürlich äußerte sie: daß sie von den Blumen, wenn sie noch im Garten oder im Topfe wachsen, recht erfreut werde, daß hingegen ein leises Schmerzgefühl, traumhaft beängstigend, ihre Brust durch-zittere, wenn sie eine abgebrochene Blume sehe – da eine solche doch eigentlich eine Leiche sei, und so eine gebrochene, zarte Blumenleiche ihre welkes Köpfchen recht traurig herab hängen lasse, wie ein totes Kind. Die Dame war fast erschrocken über

was the guilty cause of my neglecting my fair lady, and now, with mother and friend, she stood before the door, about to step into her carriage. I had scarcely time to hurry to her and assure her that it was cold. She seemed piqued at my not coming sooner, but I soon drove the clouds from her fair brow by presenting to her a beautiful flower, which I had plucked the day before, at the risk of breaking my neck, from a steep precipice. The mother inquired the name of the flower, as if it seemed to her not altogether correct that her daughter should place a strange, unknown flower before her bosom—for this was in fact the enviable position which the flower attained, and of which it could never have dreamed the day before, when on its lonely height. The silent friend here opened his mouth, and after counting the stamina of the flower, dryly remarked that it belonged to the eighth class.

It vexes me every time, when I remember that even the dear flowers which God hath made have been, like us, divided into castes, and like us are distinguished by those external names which indicate descent and family. If there must be such divisions, it were better to adopt those suggested by Theophrastus,[114] who wished that flowers might be divided according to souls— that is, their perfumes. As for myself, I have my own system of Natural Science, according to which all things are divided into those which may—or may not be—eaten!

The secret and mysterious nature of flowers was, however, anything but a secret to the elder lady, and she involuntarily remarked that she felt happy in her very soul when she saw flowers growing in the garden or in a room, while a faint, dreamy sense of pain invariably affected her on beholding a beautiful flower with broken stalk—that it was really a dead body, and that the delicate pale head of such a flower-corpse hung down like that of a dead infant. The lady here became

den trüben Widerschein ihrer Bemerkung, und es war meine Pflicht, denselben mit einigen Voltaireschen Versen zu verscheuchen. Wie doch ein paar französische Worte uns gleich in die gehörige Konvenienzstimmung zurück versetzen können! Wir lachten, Hände wurden geküßt, huldreich wurde gelächelt, die Pferde wieherten und der Wagen holperte, langsam und beschwerlich, den Berg hinunter.

Nun machten auch die Studenten Anstalt zum Abreisen, die Ranzen wurden geschnürt, die Rechnungen, die über alle Erwartung billig ausfielen, berichtigt; die empfänglichen Hausmädchen, auf deren Gesichtern die Spuren glücklicher Liebe, brachten, wie gebräuchlich ist, die Brockensträußchen, halfen solche auf die Mützen befestigen, wurden dafür mit einigen Küssen oder Groschen honoriert; und so stiegen wir alle den Berg hinab, indem die einen, wobei der Schweizer und Greifswalder, den Weg nach Schierke einschlugen, und die andern, ungefähr zwanzig Mann, wobei auch meine Landsleute und ich, angeführt von einem Wegweiser, durch die sogenannten Schneelöcher hinab zogen nach Ilsenburg.

Das ging über Hals und Kopf. Hallesche Studenten marschieren schneller als die östreichische Landwehr. Ehe ich mich dessen versah, war die kahle Partie des Berges mit den darauf zerstreuten Steingruppen schon hinter uns, und wir kamen durch einen Tannenwald, wie ich ihn den Tag vorher gesehen. Die Sonne goß schon ihre festlichen Strahlen herab und beleuchtete die humoristisch buntgekleideten Burschen, die so munter durch das Dickicht drangen, hier verschwanden, dort wieder zum Vorschein kamen, bei Sumpfstellen über die quergelegten Baumstämme liefen, bei abschüssigen Tiefen an den rankenden Wurzeln kletterten, in den ergötzlichsten Tonarten empor johlten, und eben so lustige Antwort zurück erhielten von den zwitschernden Waldvögeln, von den rauschenden Tannen, von den unsichtbar plätschernden Quellen und von dem schallenden Echo. Wenn frohe Jugend und schöne Natur zusammen kom-

alarmed at the sorrowful impression which her remark caused, and I flew to the rescue with a few Voltairian verses. How quickly two or three French words bring us back into the conventional concert pitch of conversation. We laughed, hands were kissed, gracious smiles beamed, the horses neighed, and the wagon jolted heavily and slowly adown the hill.

And now the students prepared to depart. Knapsacks were buckled, the bills, which were moderate beyond all expectation, were settled, the too susceptible housemaids, upon whose pretty countenances the traces of successful amours were plainly visible, brought, as is their custom, their Brocken bouquets, and helped some to adjust their caps; for all of Which they were duly rewarded with either coppers or kisses. Thus we all went down hill, albeit one party, among whom were the Swiss and Greifswalder, took the road towards Schierke, and the other of about twenty men, among whom were my land's people and I, led by a guide, went through the so-called Snow Holes, down to Ilsenburg.

Such a head over heels, break-neck piece of business! Halle students travel quicker than the Austrian militia. Ere I knew where I was, the bald summit of the mountain with groups of stones strewed over it was behind us, and we went through the firwood which I had seen the day before. The sun poured down a cheerful light on the merry Burschen as they merrily pressed onward through the wood, disappearing here, coming to light again there, running in marshy places across on shaking trunks of trees, climbing over shelving steeps by grasping the projecting tree roots, while they trilled all the time in the merriest manner.

men, so freuen sie sich wechselseitig. Je tiefer wir hinab stiegen, desto lieblicher rauschte das unterirdische Gewässer, nur hier und da, unter Gestein und Gestrippe, blinkte es hervor, und schien heimlich zu lauschen, ob es ans Licht treten dürfe, und endlich kam eine kleine Welle entschlossen hervor gesprungen. Nun zeigt sich die gewöhnliche Erscheinung: ein Kühner macht den Anfang, und der große Troß der Zagenden wird plötzlich, zu seinem eigenen Erstaunen, von Mut ergriffen, und eilt, sich mit jenem ersten zu vereinigen. Eine Menge anderer Quellen hüpften jetzt hastig aus ihrem Versteck, verbanden sich mit der zuerst hervorgesprungenen, und bald bildeten sie zusammen ein schon bedeutendes Bächlein, das in unzähligen Wasserfällen, und in wunderlichen Windungen, das Bergtal hinab rauscht. Das ist nun die Ilse, die liebliche, süße Ilse. Sie zieht sich durch das gesegnete Ilsetal, an dessen beiden Seiten sich die Berge allmählig höher erheben, und diese sind, bis zu ihrem Fuße, meistens mit Buchen, Eichen und gewöhnlichem Blattgesträuche bewachsen, nicht mehr mit Tannen und anderm Nadelholz. Denn jene Blätterholzart wird vorherrschend auf dem »Unterharze«, wie man die Ostseite des Brockens nennt, im Gegensatz zur Westseite desselben, die der »Oberharz« heißt, und wirklich viel höher ist und also auch viel geeigneter zum Gedeihen der Nadelhölzer.

Es ist unbeschreibbar, mit welcher Fröhlichkeit, Naivetät und Anmut die Ilse sich hinunter stürzt über die abenteuerlich gebildeten Felsstücke, die sie in ihrem Laufe findet, so daß das Wasser hier wild empor zischt oder schäumend überläuft, dort aus allerlei Steinspalten, wie aus tollen Gießkannen, in reinen Bögen sich ergießt, und unten wieder über die kleinen Steine hintrippelt, wie ein munteres Mädchen. Ja, die Sage ist wahr, die Ilse ist eine Prinzessin, die lachend und blühend den Berg hinab läuft. Wie blinkt im Sonnenschein ihr weißes Schaumgewand! Wie flattern im Winde ihre silbernen Busenbänder!

The lower we descended, the more delightfully did subterranean waters ripple around us; only here and there they peeped out amid rocks and bushes, appearing to be reconnoitering if they might yet come to light, until at last one little spring jumped forth boldly. Then followed the usual show—the bravest one makes a beginning, and then the great multitude of hesitators, suddenly inspired with courage, rush forth to join the first. A multitude of springs now leaped in haste from their ambush, united with the leader, and finally formed quite an important brook, which with its innumerable waterfalls and beautiful windings ripples adown the valley. This is now the Ilse—the sweet, pleasant Ilse. She flows through the blest Ilse vale, on whose sides the mountains gradually rise higher and higher, being clad even to their base with beech-trees, oaks, and the usual shrubs, the firs and other needle-covered evergreens having disappeared. For that variety of trees prevails upon the Lower Harz, as the east side of the Brocken is called in contradistinction to the West side or Upper Harz, being really much higher and better adapted to the growth of evergreens.

No pen can describe the merriment, simplicity, and gentleness with which the Ilse leaps or glides amid the wildly piled rocks which rise in her path, so that the water strangely whizzes or foams in one place amid rifted rocks, and in another wells through a thousand crannies, as if from a giant watering-pot, and then in collected stream trips away over the pebbles like a merry maiden. Yes, the old legend is true, the Ilse is a princess, who laughing in beauty runs adown the mountain. How her white foam garment gleams in the sunshine! How her silvered scarf flutters in the breeze! How her diamonds flash! The high beech-tree gazes down on her like a grave father secretly smiling at the capricious self-will of a

Wie funkeln und blitzen ihre Diamanten! Die hohen Buchen
stehen dabei gleich ernsten Vätern, die verstohlen lächelnd dem
Mutwillen des lieblichen Kindes zusehen; die weißen Birken
bewegen sich tantenhaft vergnügt, und doch zugleich ängstlich über die gewagten Sprünge; der stolze Eichbaum schaut
drein wie ein verdrießlicher Oheim, der das schöne Wetter be-
zahlen soll; die Vögelein in den Lüften jubeln ihren Beifall, die
Blumen am Ufer flüstern zärtlich: O, nimm uns mit, nimm
uns mit, lieb Schwesterchen! – aber das lustige Mädchen springt
unaufhaltsam weiter, und plötzlich ergreift sie den träumenden
Dichter, und es strömt auf mich herab ein Blumenregen von
klingenden Strahlen und strahlenden Klängen, und die Sinne
vergehen mir vor lauter Herrlichkeit, und ich höre nur noch
die flötensüße Stimme:

Ich bin die Prinzessin Ilse,
Und wohne im Ilsenstein;
Komm mit nach meinem Schlosse,
Wir wollen selig sein.

Dein Haupt will ich benetzen
Mit meiner klaren Well,
Du sollst deine Schmerzen vergessen,
Du sorgenkranker Gesell!

In meinen weißen Armen,
An meiner weißen Brust,
Da sollst du liegen und träumen
Von alter Märchenlust.

Ich will dich küssen und herzen,
Wie ich geherzt und geküßt
Den lieben Kaiser Heinrich,
Der nun gestorben ist.

Es bleiben tot die Toten,
Und nur der Lebendige lebt;

darling child, the white birch-trees nod their beads around like delighted aunts, the proud oak looks on like a not over-pleased uncle, as though he must pay for all the fine weather; the birds in the air sing their share in their joy, the flowers on the bank whisper, "Oh, take us with thee! take us with thee! dear sister!" but the wild maiden may not be withheld, and she leaps onward, and suddenly seizes the dreaming poet, and there streams over me a flower rain of ringing gleams and flashing tones, and all my senses are lost in beauty and splendor as I hear only the voice sweet pealing as a flute.

I am the Princess Ilse,[115]
And dwell in Ilsenstein;
Come with me to my castle,
Thou shalt be blest—and mine!

With ever-flowing fountains
I'll cool thy weary brow;
Thou'lt lose amid their rippling,
The cares which grieve thee now.

In my white arms reposing
And on my snow-white breast
Thou'lt dream of old, old legends,
And sink in joy to rest.

I'll kiss thee and caress thee,
As in the ancient day
I kissed the Emperor Henry,
Who long has passed away.

The dead are dead and silent
Only the living love;

Und ich bin schön und blühend,
Mein lachendes Herze bebt.

Komm in mein Schloß herunter,
In mein kristallenes Schloß,
Da tanzen die Fräulein und Ritter,
Es jubelt der Knappentroß.

Es rauschen die seidenen Schleppen,
Es klirren die Eisensporn,
Die Zwerge trompeten und pauken,
Und fiedeln und blasen das Horn.

Doch dich soll mein Arm umschlingen,
Wie er Kaiser Heinrich umschlang;
Ich hielt ihm zu die Ohren,
Wenn die Trompet erklang.

Unendlich selig ist das Gefühl, wenn die Erscheinungswelt
mit unserer Gemütswelt zusammenrinnt, und grüne Bäume,
Gedanken, Vögelgesang, Wehmut, Himmelsbläue, Erinnerung
und Kräuterduft sich in süßen Arabesken verschlingen. Die
Frauen kennen am besten dieses Gefühl, und darum mag auch
ein so holdselig ungläubiges Lächeln um ihre Lippen schweben,
wenn wir mit Schulstolz unsere logischen Taten rühmen, wie
wir alles so hübsch eingeteilt in objektiv und subjektiv, wie wir
unsere Köpfe apothekenartig mit tausend Schubladen versehen,
wo in der einen Vernunft, in der andern Verstand, in der dritten
Witz, in der vierten schlechter Witz, und in der fünften gar
nichts, nämlich die Idee, enthalten ist.

Wie im Traume fortwandelnd, hatte ich fast nicht bemerkt,
daß wir die Tiefe des Ilsetals verlassen, und wieder bergauf
stiegen. Dies ging sehr steil und mühsam, und mancher von
uns kam außer Atem. Doch wie unser seliger Vetter, der zu
Mölln begraben liegt, dachten wir im Voraus ans Bergabsteigen,
und waren um so vergnügter. Endlich gelangten wir auf den
Ilsenstein.

And I am fair and blooming
—Dost feel my wild heart move?

And as my heart is beating,
My crystal castle rings;
Where many a knight and lady
In merry measure springs.

Silk trains are softly rustling,
Spurs ring from night to morn;
And dwarfs are gaily drumming,
And blow the golden horn.

As round the Emperor Henry,
My arms round thee shall fall;
I held his ears—he heard not
The trumpet's warning call.

We feel infinite happiness when the outer world blends with the
world of our own soul, and green trees, thoughts, the songs of
birds, gentle melancholy, the blue of heaven, memory, and the
perfume of flowers run together in sweet arabesques.[116] Women
best understand this feeling, and this may be the cause that such
a sweet, incredulous smile plays around their lips when we, with
school pride, boast of our logical deeds, how we have classified
everything so nicely into subjective and objective, how our beads
are provided, apothecary-like, with a thousand drawers, one of
which contains reason, another understanding, a third wretched
wit, and the fifth nothing at all—that is to say, the Idea.[117]

As if wandering in dreams, I scarcely observed that we had left
the depths of the Ilsethal and were now again climbing up hill.
This was steep and difficult work, and many of us lost our
breath. But like our late lamented cousin, who now lies buried at
Mölln,[118] we constantly kept in mind the ease with which we

129

Das ist ein ungeheurer Granitfelsen, der sich lang und keck aus der Tiefe erhebt. Von drei Seiten umschließen ihn die hohen, waldbedeckten Berge, aber die vierte, die Nordseite, ist frei, und hier schaut man das unten liegende Ilsenburg und die Ilse, weit hinab ins niedere Land. Auf der turmartigen Spitze des Felsens steht ein großes, eisernes Kreuz, und zur Not ist da noch Platz für vier Menschenfüße.

Wie nun die Natur, durch Stellung und Form, den Ilsenstein mit phantastischen Reizen geschmückt, so hat auch die Sage ihren Rosenschein darüber ausgegossen. Gottschalk berichtet: »Man erzählt, hier habe ein verwünschtes Schloß gestanden, in welchem die reiche, schöne Prinzessin Ilse gewohnt, die sich noch jetzt jeden Morgen in der Ilse bade; und wer so glücklich ist, den rechten Zeitpunkt zu treffen, werde von ihr in den Felsen, wo ihr Schloß sei, geführt und königlich belohnt!« Andere erzählen von der Liebe des Fräuleins Ilse und des Ritters von Westenberg eine hübsche Geschichte, die einer unserer bekanntesten Dichter romantisch in der »Abendzeitung« besungen hat. Andere wieder erzählen anders: es soll der altsächsische Kaiser Heinrich gewesen sein, der mit Ilse, der schönen Wasserfee, in ihrer verzauberten Felsenburg die kaiserlichsten Stunden genossen. Ein neuerer Schriftsteller, Herr Niemann, Wohlgeb., der ein Harzreisebuch geschrieben, worin er die Gebirgshöhen, Abweichungen der Magnetnadel, Schulden der Städte und dergleichen mit löblichem Fleiße und genauen Zahlen angegeben, behauptet indes: »Was man von der Prinzessin Ilse erzählt, gehört dem Fabelreiche an.« So sprechen alle diese Leute, denen eine solche Prinzessin niemals erschienen ist, wir aber, die wir von schönen Damen besonders begünstigt werden, wissen das besser. Auch Kaiser Heinrich wußte es. Nicht umsonst hingen die altsächsischen Kaiser so sehr an ihrem heimischen Harze. Man blättere nur in der hübschen Lüneburger Chronik, wo die guten, alten Herren in wunderlich treuherzigen Holzschnitten abkonterfeit sind, wohlgeharnischt, hoch auf ihrem gewapp-

should descend, and were much the better off in consequence. Finally we reached the Ilsenstein.

This is an enormous granite rock, which rises high and boldly from a glen. On three sides it is surrounded by woody hills, but from the fourth—the north—there is an open view, and we gaze upon the Ilsenburg and the Ilse lying far below, and our glances wander beyond into the lower land. On the tower-like summit of the rock stands a great iron cross, and in case of need there is also here a resting-place for four human feet.

As nature, through picturesque position and form, has adorned the Ilsenstein with strange and beautiful charms, so has also Legend poured over it her rosy light. According to Gott-schalk, "the people say that there once stood here an enchanted castle, in which dwelt the fair Princess Ilse, who yet bathes every morning in the Ilse. He who is so fortunate as to hit upon the exact time and place, will be led by her into the rock, where her castle lies, and receive a royal reward." Others narrate a pleasant legend of the loves of the Lady Ilse and of the Knight of Westenberg,[119] which has been romantically sung by one of our most noted poets, in the *Evening Journal*. Others again say that it was the old Saxon Emperor Henry, who passed in pleasure his imperial hours with the water-nymph, Ilse, in her enchanted castle. A later author, one Niemann, Esq.,[120] who has written a Harz Guide, in which the heights of the hills, variations of the compass, town finances, and similar matters are described with praiseworthy accuracy, asserts, however, that "what is narrated of the Princess Ilse belongs entirely to the realm of fable." So all men, to whom a beautiful princess has never appeared, assert; but we who have been especially favored by fair ladies know better. And this the Emperor Henry knew too! It was not without cause that the old Saxon emperors held so firmly to their native Harz. Let any one only turn over the leaves of the fair *Lüneburg*

neten Schlachtroß, die heilige Kaiserkrone auf dem teuren
Haupte, Szepter und Schwert in festen Händen; und auf den
lieben, knebelbärtigen Gesichtern kann man deutlich lesen, wie
oft sie sich nach den süßen Herzen ihrer Harzprinzessinnen und
dem traulichen Rauschen der Harzwälder zurück sehnten, wenn
sie in der Fremde weilten, wohl gar in dem zitronen- und gift-
reichen Welschland, wohin sie und ihre Nachfolger so oft ver-
lockt wurden von dem Wunsche, römische Kaiser zu heißen,
einer echtdeutschen Titelsucht, woran Kaiser und Reich zu
Grunde gingen.

Ich rate aber jedem, der auf der Spitze des Ilsensteins steht,
weder an Kaiser und Reich, noch an die schöne Ilse, sondern
bloß an seine Füße zu denken. Denn als ich dort stand, in Gedanken verloren, hörte ich plötzlich die unterirdische Musik des
Zauberschlosses, und ich sah, wie sich die Berge ringsum auf
die Köpfe stellten, und die roten Ziegeldächer zu Ilsenburg an-
fingen zu tanzen, und die grünen Bäume in der blauen Luft
herum flogen, daß es mir blau und grün vor den Augen wurde,
und ich sicher, vom Schwindel erfaßt, in den Abgrund gestürzt
wäre, wenn ich mich nicht, in meiner Seelennot, ans eiserne
Kreuz festgeklammert hätte. Daß ich, in so mißlicher Stellung,
dieses letztere getan habe, wird mir gewiß niemand verdenken.

Die »Harzreise« ist und bleibt Fragment, und die bunten Fä-
den, die so hübsch hineingesponnen sind, um sich im Ganzen
harmonisch zu verschlingen, werden plötzlich, wie von der
Schere der unerbittlichen Parze, abgeschnitten. Vielleicht ver-
webe ich sie weiter in künftigen Liedern, und was jetzt kärg-
lich verschwiegen ist, wird alsdann vollauf gesagt. Am Ende
kommt es auch auf eins heraus, wann und wo man etwas ausgesprochen hat, wenn man es nur überhaupt einmal ausspricht.
Mögen die eizelnen Werke immerhin Fragmente bleiben, wenn
sie nur in ihrer Vereinigung ein Ganzes bilden. Durch solche

Chronicle,[121] where the good old gentlemen are represented in wondrously true-hearted woodcuts as well weaponed, high on their mailed war steeds; the holy imperial crown on their blessed heads, scepter and sword in firm hands; and then in their dear bearded faces he can plainly read how they often longed for the sweet hearts of their Harz princesses, and for the familiar rustling of the Harz forests—when they lingered in distant lands. Yes, even when in the orange and poison gifted Italy, whither they, with their followers, were often enticed by the desire of becoming Roman emperors—a genuine German lust for title which finally destroyed emperor and realm.

I, however, advise every one who may hereafter stand on the summit of the Ilsenburg to think neither of emperor and crown, nor of the fair Ilse, but simply of his own feet. For as I stood there, lost in thought, I suddenly heard the subterranean music of the enchanted castle, and saw the mountains around begin to stand on their heads, while the red-tiled roofs of Ilsenburg were dancing, and green trees flew through the air, until all was green and blue before my eyes, and I, overcome by giddiness, would assuredly have fallen into the abyss, had I not, in the dire need of my soul, clung fast to the iron cross. No one who reflects on the critically ticklish situation in which I was then placed, can possibly find fault with me for having done this.[122]

The "Harz Journey" is, and remains, a fragment, and the variegated threads which were so neatly wound through it, with the intention to bind it into a harmonious whole, have been suddenly snapped asunder as if by the shears of the implacable Destinies. It may be that I will one day weave them into new songs, and that that which is now stingily withheld, will then be spoken in full. But when or what we have spoken will all come to one and

Vereinigung mag hier und da das Mangelhafte ergänzt, das Schroffe ausgeglichen und das Allzuherbe gemildert werden. Dieses würde vielleicht schon bei den ersten Blättern der »Harzreise« der Fall sein, und sie könnten wohl einen minder sauern Eindruck hervorbringen, wenn man anderweitig erführe, daß der Unmut, den ich gegen Göttingen im allgemeinen hege, obschon er noch größer ist, als ich ihn ausgesprochen, doch lange nicht so groß ist wie die Verehrung, die ich für einige Individuen dort empfinde. Und warum sollte ich es verschweigen, ich meine hier ganz besonders jenen viel teuern Mann, der schon in frühern Zeiten sich so freundlich meiner annahm, mir schon damals eine innige Liebe für das Studium der Geschichte einflößte, mich späterhin in dem Eifer für dasselbe bestärkte, und dadurch meinen Geist auf ruhigere Bahnen führte, meinem Lebensmute heilsamere Richtungen anwies, und mir überhaupt jene historischen Tröstungen bereitete, ohne welche ich die qualvollen Erscheinungen des Tages nimmermehr ertragen würde. Ich spreche von Georg Sartorius, dem großen Geschichtsforscher und Menschen, dessen Auge ein klarer Stern ist in unserer dunkeln Zeit, und dessen gastliches Herz offen steht für alle fremde Leiden und Freuden, für die Besorgnisse des Bettlers und des Königs, und für die letzten Seufzer untergehender Völker und ihrer Götter. –

Ich kann nicht umhin, hier ebenfalls anzudeuten: daß der Oberharz, jener Teil des Harzes, den ich bis zum Anfang des Ilsetals beschrieben habe, bei weitem keinen so erfreulichen Anblick wie der romantisch malerische Unterharz gewährt, und in seiner wildschroffen, tannendüstern Schönheit gar sehr mit demselben kontrastiert; so wie ebenfalls die drei, von der Ilse, von der Bode und von der Selke gebildeten Täler des Unterharzes gar anmutig unter einander kontrastieren, wenn man den Charakter jedes Tales zu personifizieren weiß. Es sind drei Frauengestalten, wovon man nicht so leicht zu entscheiden vermag, welche die schönste sei.

the same thing at last, provided that we do but speak. The single works may ever remain fragments, if they only form a whole by their union. By such a connection the defective may here and there be supplied, the rough be polished down, and that which is altogether too harsh be modified and softened. This is perhaps especially applicable to the first pages of the "Harz Journey," and they would in all probability have caused a far less unfavorable impression could the reader in some other place have learned that the ill humor which I entertain for Göttingen in general, although greater than I have here expressed it, is still far from being equal to the respect which I entertain for certain individuals there. And why should I conceal the fact that I here allude particularly to that estimable man, who in earlier years received me so kindly, inspiring me even then with a deep love for the study of History; who strengthened my zeal for it later in life and thus led my soul to calmer paths; who indicated to my peculiar disposition its peculiar paths, and who finally gave me those historical consolations, without which I should never have been able to support the painful events of the present day. I speak of Georg Sartorius,[123] the great investigator of history and of humanity, whose eye is a bright star in our dark times, and whose hospitable heart is ever open to all the griefs and joys of others—for the needs of the beggar or the king, and for the last sighs of nations perishing with their gods.

I cannot here refrain from remarking that the Upper Harz—that portion of which I described as far as the beginning of the Ilsethal—did not by any means make so favorable an impression on me as the romantic and picturesque Lower Harz, and in its wild dark fir-tree beauty contrasts strangely with the other, just as the three valleys formed by the Ilse, the Bode and the Selke, beautifully contrast with each other when we are able to individualize the character of each. They are three beautiful women of whom it is impossible to determine which is the fairest.

Von der lieben, süßen Ilse und wie süß und lieblich sie mich empfangen, habe ich schon gesagt und gesungen. Die düstere Schöne, die Bode, empfing mich nicht so gnädig, und als ich sie im schmiededunkeln Rübeland zuerst erblickte, schien sie gar mürrisch und verhüllte sich in einen silbergrauen Regenschleier. Aber mit rascher Liebe warf sie ihn ab, als ich auf die Höhe der Roßtrappe gelangte, ihr Antlitz leuchtete mir entgegen in sonnigster Pracht, aus allen Zügen hauchte eine kolossale Zärtlichkeit, und aus der bezwungenen Felsenbrust drang es hervor wie Sehnsuchtseufzer und schmelzende Laute der Wehmut. Minder zärtlich, aber fröhlicher, zeigte sich mir die schöne Selke, die schöne, liebenswürdige Dame, deren edle Einfalt und heitre Ruhe alle sentimentale Familiarität entfernt hält, die aber doch durch ein halbverstecktes Lächeln ihren neckenden Sinn verrät; und diesem möchte ich es wohl zuschreiben, daß mich im Selketal gar mancherlei kleines Ungemach heimsuchte, daß ich, indem ich über das Wasser springen wollte, just in die Mitte hineinplumpste, daß nachher, als ich das nasse Fußzeug mit Pantoffeln vertauscht hatte, einer derselben mir abhanden oder vielmehr abfüßen kam, daß mir ein Windstoß die Mütze entführte, daß mir Walddorne die Beine zerfetzten, u. leider s. w. Doch all dieses Ungemach verzeihe ich gern der schönen Dame, denn sie ist schön. Und jetzt steht sie vor meiner Einbildung mit all ihrem stillen Liebreiz, und scheint zu sagen: wenn ich auch lache, so meine ich es doch gut mit Ihnen, und ich bitte Sie, besingen Sie mich. Die herrliche Bode tritt ebenfalls hervor in meiner Erinnerung, und ihr dunkles Auge spricht: du gleichst mir im Stolz und im Schmerze, und ich will, daß du mich liebst. Auch die schöne Ilse kommt herangesprungen, zierlich und bezaubernd in Miene, Gestalt und Bewegung; sie gleicht ganz dem holden Wesen, das meine Träume beseligt, und ganz wie Sie, schaut sie mich an, mit unwiderstehlicher Gleichgültigkeit und doch zugleich so innig, so ewig, so durchsichtig wahr –
Nun, ich bin Paris, die drei Göttinnen stehen vor mir, und

I have already spoken and sung of the fair, sweet Ilse, and how sweetly and kindly she received me. The darker beauty, the Bode, was not so gracious in her reception, and as I beheld her in the smithy-dark Turnip land, she appeared me to be altogether ill-natured and hid herself beneath a silver-gray rain veil; but with impatient love she suddenly threw it off, as I ascended the summit of the Rosstrappe her countenance gleamed upon me with the sunniest splendor, from every feature beamed the tenderness of a giantess, and from the agitated, rocky bosom there was a sound as of sighs of deep longing and melting tones of woe. Less tender, but far merrier, did I find the pretty Selke, an amiable lady whose noble simplicity and calm repose[124] held at a distance all sentimental familiarity, but who by a half-concealed smile betrayed her mocking mood. It was perhaps to this secret, merry spirit that I might have attributed the many "little miseries" which beset me in the Selkethal—as, for instance, when I sought to spring over the rivulet, I plunged in exactly up to my middle; how when I continued my wet campaign with slippers, one of them was soon "not at hand," or rather "not at foot," for I lost it; how a puff of wind bore away my cap; how thorns scratched me, etc., etc. Yet do I forgive the fair lady all this, for she is fair. And even now she stands before the gates of Imagination, in all her silent loveliness, and seems to say, "Though I laugh I mean no harm, and I pray you sing of ne!" The magnificent Bode also sweeps into my memory, and her dark eye says, "Thou art like me in pride and in pain, and I will that thou lovest me." Also the fair Ilse comes merrily springing, delicate and fascinating in mien, form, and motion, in all things like the dear being who blesses my dreams, and like her she gazes on me with unconquerable indifference, and is withal so deeply, so eternally, so manifestly true. Well, I am Paris, and I award the apple to the fair Ilse.

den Apfel gebe ich der schönen Ilse.

Es ist heute der erste Mai. Wie ein Meer des Lebens ergießt sich der Frühling über die Erde, der weiße Blütenschaum bleibt an den Bäumen hängen, ein weiter, warmer Nebelglanz verbreitet sich überall. In der Stadt blitzen freudig die Fensterscheiben der Häuser, an den Dächern bauen die Spatzen wieder ihre Nestchen, auf der Straße wandeln die Leute und wundern sich, daß die Luft so angreifend und ihnen selbst so wunderlich zu Mute ist; die bunten Vierlanderinnen bringen Veilchensträußer; die Waisenkinder, mit ihren blauen Jäckchen und ihren lieben, unehelichen Gesichtchen, ziehen über den Jungfernstieg und freuen sich, als sollten sie heute einen Vater wiederfinden; der Bettler an der Brücke schaut so vergnügt, als hätte er das große Los gewonnen, sogar den schwarzen, noch ungehenkten Makler, der dort mit seinem spitzbübischen Manufakturwaren-Gesicht einherläuft, bescheint die Sonne mit ihren tolerantesten Strahlen, – ich will hinauswandern vor das Tor.

Es ist der erste Mai, und ich denke deiner, du schöne Ilse – oder soll ich dich »Agnes« nennen, weil dir dieser Name am besten gefällt? – ich denke deiner, und ich möchte wieder zusehen, wie du leuchtend den Berg hinabläufst. Am liebsten aber möchte ich unten im Tale stehen und dich auffangen in meine Arme. – Es ist ein schöner Tag! Überall sehe ich die grüne Farbe, die Farbe der Hoffnung. Überall, wie holde Wunder, blühen hervor die Blumen, und auch mein Herz will wieder blühen. Dieses Herz ist auch eine Blume, eine gar wunderliche.

Es ist kein bescheidenes Veilchen, keine lachende Rose, keine reine Lilie, oder sonstiges Blümchen, das mit artiger Lieblichkeit den Mädchensinn erfreut, und sich hübsch vor den hübschen Busen stecken läßt, und heute welkt und morgen wieder blüht. Dieses Herz gleicht mehr jener schweren, abenteuerlichen Blume aus den Wäldern Brasiliens, die, der Sage nach, alle hundert Jahre nur einmal blüht. Ich erinnere mich, daß ich als Knabe eine solche Blume gesehen. Wir hörten in der Nacht einen

It is the first of May, and spring is pouring like a sea of life over the earth, a foam of white blossoms covers the trees, the glass in the town windows flashes merrily, swallows are again building on the roofs, people saunter along the street, wondering that the air affects them so much, and that they feel so cheerful; the oddly dressed Vierlander[125] girls are selling bouquets of violets, foundling children, with their blue jackets and dear little illegitimate faces, run along the Jungfernstieg, as happily as if they had all found their fathers; the beggar on the bridge looks as jolly as though he had won the first lottery prize, and even on the grimy and as yet unhung pedler, who scours about with his rascally "manufactory goods" countenance, the sun shines with his best-natured rays—I will take a walk beyond the town gate.

It is the first of May, and I think of thee, thou fair Ilse—or shall I call thee by the name which I better love, of Agnes? I think of thee and would fain see once more how thou leapest in light adown thy hill. But best of all were it could I stand in the valley below, and hold thee in my arms. It is a lovely day! Green—the color of hope—is everywhere around me. Everywhere flowers—those dear wonders—are blooming, and my heart will bloom again also. This heart is also a flower of strange and wondrous sort. It is no modest violet, no smiling rose, no pure lily, or similar flower, which with good gentle loveliness makes glad a maiden's soul, and may be fitly placed before her pretty breast, and which withers to-day, and to-morrow blooms again.[127] No, this heart rather resembles that strange, heavy flower, from the woods of Brazil, which, according to the legend, blooms but once in a century. I remember well that I once, when a boy, saw such a flower. During the night we heard an explosion, as of a pistol, and the next morning a neighbor's children told me that it was their "aloe," which had bloomed

139

Schuß, wie von einer Pistole, und am folgenden Morgen erzählten mir die Nachbarskinder, daß es ihre »Aloe« gewesen,
die mit solchem Knalle plötzlich aufgeblüht sei. Sie führten
mich in ihren Garten, und da sah ich, zu meiner Verwunderung,
daß das niedrige, harte Gewächs mit den närrisch breiten,
scharfgezackten Blättern, woran man sich leicht verletzen
konnte, jetzt ganz in die Höhe geschossen war, und oben, wie
eine goldene Krone, die herrlichste Blüte trug. Wir Kinder
konnten nicht so hoch hinaufsehen, und der alte, schmunzelnde
Christian, der uns lieb hatte, baute eine hölzerne Treppe um die
Blume herum, und da kletterten wir hinauf, wie die Katzen,
und schauten neugierig in den offenen Blumenkelch, woraus
die gelben Strahlenfäden und wildfremden Düfte mit un-
erhörter Pracht hervordrangen.

Ja, Agnes, oft und leicht kommt dieses Herz nicht zum Blühen; so viel ich mich erinnere, hat es nur ein einziges Mal ge-
blüht, und das mag schon lange her sein, gewiß schon hundert
Jahr. Ich glaube, so herrlich auch damals seine Blüte sich ent-
faltete, so mußte sie doch aus Mangel an Sonnenschein und
Wärme elendiglich verkümmern, wenn sie nicht gar von einem
dunkeln Wintersturme gewaltsam zerstört worden. Jetzt aber
regt und drängt es sich wieder in meiner Brust, und hörst du
plötzlich den Schuß – Mädchen, erschrick nicht! ich hab mich
nicht tot geschossen, sondern meine Liebe sprengt ihre Knospe,
und schießt empor in strahlenden Liedern, in ewigen Dithy-
ramben, in freudigster Sangesfülle.

Ist dir aber diese hohe Liebe zu hoch, Mädchen, so mach es
dir bequem, und besteige die hölzerne Treppe, und schaue von
dieser hinab in mein blühendes Herz.

Es ist noch früh am Tage, die Sonne hat kaum die Hälfte
ihres Weges zurückgelegt, und mein Herz duftet schon so stark,
daß es mir betäubend zu Kopfe steigt, daß ich nicht mehr weiß,
wo die Ironie aufhört und der Himmel anfängt, daß ich die
Luft mit meinen Seufzern bevölkere, und daß ich selbst wieder

with the shot. They led me to their garden, where I saw to my astonishment that the low, hard plant, with ridiculously broad, sharp-pointed leaves, which were capable of inflicting wounds, had shot high in the air and bore aloft beautiful flowers, like a golden crown. We children could not see so high, and the old grinning Christian, who liked us all so well, built a wooden stair around the flower, upon which we scrambled like cats, and gazed curiously into the open calyx, from which yellow threads, like rays of light, and strange foreign odors, pressed forth in unheard-of splendor.

Yes, Agnes, this flower blooms not often, not without effort; and according to my recollection it has as yet opened but once, and that must have been long ago—certainly at least a century since. And I believe that, gloriously as it then unfolded its blossoms, it must now miserably pine for want of sunshine and warmth, if it is not indeed shattered by some mighty wintry storm. But now it moves, and swells, and bursts in my bosom— dost thou hear the explosion? Maiden, be not terrified! I have not shot myself, but my love has burst its bud and shoots upwards in gleaming songs, in eternal dithyrambs, in the most joyful fulness of poesy!

But if this high love has grown too high, then, young lady, take it comfortably, climb the wooden steps, and look from them down into my blooming heart.

It is as yet early; the sun has hardly left half his road behind him, and my heart already breathes forth so powerfully its perfumed vapor that it bewilders my brain, and I no longer know where iron ceases and heaven begins, or that I people the air with my sighs, and that I myself would fain dissolve into sweet atoms in the uncreated Divinity—how will it be when night comes on, and the stars shine out in heaven, "the unlucky stars who could tell thee—"

zerrinnen möchte in süße Atome, in die unerschaffene Gott-
heit; – wie soll das erst gehen, wenn es Nacht wird, und die
Sterne am Himmel erscheinen, »die unglückselgen Sterne, die
dir sagen können – –«

Es ist der erste Mai, der lumpigste Ladenschwengel hat heute
das Recht, sentimental zu werden, und dem Dichter wolltest du
es verwehren?

It is the first of May, the lowest errand boy has to-day a right to be sentimental, and would you deny the privilege to a poet ?

NOTES

1. The epigraph is taken from Ludwig Börne's commemoration of Jean Paul (*Gedenkrede auf Jean Paul*) in the Frankfurt Museum on December 2, 1825.

2. The first draft of *Harz Journey* falls between October 1824 and January 1825, and the same probably holds true for most of the five poems included in it. They were later given titles and reintroduced by Heine in 1827 as the section *Aus der Harzreise* in the *Buch der Lieder* (*Book of Songs*). This first poem was entitled *Prolog*.

3. Founded in 1737, the Georgia Augusta University (the official name of the University of Göttingen) had been the most important German university during the second half of the eighteenth century. When Heine enrolled there, the university had already outlived its glory: what remained were the old generation of academics and access to highly prestigious cultural institutions such as the library and various scientific laboratories.

4. Wilhelm Lüder was a student at Göttingen famous for his corpulence and physical strength.

5. Heine's turn of phrase alludes to those responsible for suspending and expelling students.

6. The reference here is to *Burschenschaften*, student associations. During the wars against Napoleon, the old student organizations were modernized and politicized; after the Congress of Vienna,

they became the voice of liberal and nationalistic tendencies, to the point of clashing with the political authorities. When he began his studies of law at Bonn in 1819, Heine joined the *Burschenschaft Allgemeinheit*. However, the increasing chauvinistic and anti-semitic tendencies at Göttingen eventually lead to the Jewish Heine's withdrawal from the *Burschenschaft*. In this passage, as in others of *The Harz Journey*, emerges the author's new point of view on the grotesque and nationalistic degeneration of student associations. Weenderstrasse is the main street in Göttingen.

7. Names of places outside Göttingen where members of student associations confronted each other in duels (the *Mensur*), inflicting the *Schmiß* on each other, the characteristic scar on the face.

8. Wordplay on *ordentlich* ("orderly, regular, neat") and *unordentlich* ("disorderly, dirty"), but not "extraordinary" (*ausserordentlich*).

9. Heine is referring to the genuinely pedantic topographical work *Göttingen in medizinischer, physischer und historischer Hinsicht* (*Göttingen: A Medical, Physical, and Historical Survey*), published in 1825 by Karl Friedrich Heinrich Marx. A baptized Jew, Marx was a teacher recognized by the university at Göttingen from 1822 on and primarily interested in infectious diseases, forensic medicine, and the history of medicine.

10. A beer garden where students used to gather.

11. In the 1834 and 1858 French editions of *The Harz Journey*, the name of Karl Friedrich Eichhorn (1781–1854), a famous scholar of German law, is explicitly mentioned. However, J.P. Lyser, a friend of Heine's, identifies the scholar—with a closer approximation to the truth, given the tone of the passage—with the extremely erudite naturalist Johann Friedrich Blumenbach.

12. In the patriotic, anti-Napoleonic climate and in the context of the law studies initiated by Friedrich Carl von Savigny, the issue of the day concerned the relations between Roman law and Germanic

law. Roman law, accepted in Germany since the XIV century, increasingly tended to assert the predominance of associative bodies as opposed to the protection of the individual. That even Heine defined Roman law as selfish (and he re-emphasized this in 1855 in *Memoiren*, where the *Corpus Juris* is called the bible of selfishness) is an extremely significant indication of how interested he was in the legal debate of the time.

13. Tribonian (d. A.D. 546), the famous jurist who made a fundamental contribution to the *Pandectae*, the codification of Roman law promoted by Justinian. Hermogenian was also a noted IV century jurist, who collected the edicts of the Emperor Constantine in the code that bears his name.

14. The intertwined hands were the trademark of a publisher who, at that time, issued a widely distributed edition of the *Corpus Juris*.

15. P.H. Schäfer and C.C. Dohrs were the two head custodians of the university at the time. Schäfer ("shepherd"), and Dohrs (modified to "Doris") humorously recall the idylls of pastoral poetry that was fashionable in the eighteenth century. Salomon Gessner is thus cited as an exemplary author, although no Doris appears in his work. Instead, Heine might have had in mind the numerous poems dedicated to Doris by Johann Wilhem Ludwig Gleim (1719-1803).

16. Typically, this had nothing to do with a Rossini aria, but rather with a popular folk song of the time.

17. The Lex Furia (in the Code of Justinian: Fusia) Canina limited the freeing of slaves provided for in a will. The connection with the maid is unclear: some commentators thus see in the student slang term used by Heine an allusion to *Fuselkanne*, a shot of third-rate schnapps, which, in a certain metaphorical sense may refer to a "loose woman."

18. It recalls the overbearing creditor of student slang, but, like the preceding Fusia Canina, it also has a mercenary erotic connotation.

19. An unclear allusion: perhaps to the blue tail-coat of Goethe's Werther, or perhaps to the blue trousers which gradually replaced *culottes* in the French Revolution.

20. This is perhaps a reference to the dialect term *bussel*: "to cover with kisses."

21. See Daniel, 4:29.

22. The translation by Leland presents here the following, additional passage: "Still it is by no means certain that this fortress would have resistvd an ass laden with gold, any more than did that of which Philip of Macedon spoke."

23. A reference to Anton Bauer (1772–1843), a famous scholar of penal law who taught at Göttingen from 1813 and contributed (from this the comparison with Lycurgus, the Spartan lawmaker) to the compilation of the penal code of Hannover. Heine attended his lectures in 1824.

24. The jurist Gustav Hugo (1764–1844), a charismatic representative of the eighteenth-century Georg August University. When Heine defended his thesis before him in July 1825, he was dean of the law faculty. The fact that Heine introduced him here as Cujacius is explained by Gustav Hugo's frequent references to Jacques Cujas (1522–1590), the founder of the humanistic-philosophical method of exegesis of the sources of Roman law.

25. Allusion to a passage in the *Corpus Juris Civilis* under the title *De Arboribus Cadendis*. It deals with the issue, controversial but marginal, of the pruning of trees placed at the line between two properties. A dispute had flared up over this point: Hugo favored pruning the top half, while Anton Thibaut, aligned against the Historical School regarding codification, opted instead for the lower half.

26. During the years of the Restoration, the figure of Prometheus became a symbol of the aspirations for freedom repressed by the

powers of the Holy Alliance. For Heine in particular, the destiny of Prometheus bound equalled that of Napoleon confinedto St. Helena: the French edition of 1858 is more explicit: "the insulting force and mute violence of the Holy Alliance have chained the hero to a rock in the ocean."

27. Not the braggart baron, but the high state functionary of Hannover, Gerlach Adolf, Baron of Münchhausen (1688–1770), who was the first guardian of the University.

28. *Befreiungskriege* (literally, "wars of liberation") was the term used by German historiography to indicate the wars waged against French occupation of German territories.

29. Caspar Friedrich Gottschalk (1772–1836) was the author of the first accredited guide to the Harz. Heine probably consulted the second edition of 1817 and not the revised one of 1823, since he vainly looked for the Cathedral in Goslar, demolished in 1819.

30. In this case, the young apprentice was a businessman from Osterode, Karl Dörne, who was highly amused when he recognized himself in this episode upon publication of *The Harz Journey*. He later wanted to give tit for tat to his travel companion by telling the story of an encounter with Heine in the Harz in the magazine *Der Gesellschafter*.

31. The story of the Duke Ernest II of Swabia (d. 1030), who had refused to sacrifice a friendship to family and state interests, had been the object of numerous literary elaborations since medieval times.

32. In the dubious poems of Ossian, reworked and published by James Macpherson in 1765, the shades of the dead are transparent.

33. It is a very popular *Volkslied* transcribed in the collection *Sammlung deutscher Volkslieder,* published in 1807 by Johann Gustav Büsching and Friedrich Heinrich von der Hagen.

34. Wordplay between Klärchen's song in Goethe's *Egmont* [*Freudvoll / Und leidvoll, / Gedankenvoll sein* (Rejoicing and suffering, absorbed in thought)] and a *Volkslied* from Hessen [*Die Gedanken sind frei / Wer kann sie erraten* (Thoughts are free, who can guess them)] which during the course of the nineteenth century assumed a distinctly patriotic and liberal cast. The wordplay, the "corruption" of the text, is probably a satirical invention of Heine himself.

35. *Struggles at Werther's Tomb* by Karl Ernst, Baron of Reitzenstein, was the most widely distributed of the numerous sentimentalizing poems put into circulation shortly after the publication of Goethe's novel.

36. Heine is thinking of the less than conventional landscapes by E.T.A. Hoffmann. The author, greatly admired by Heine, had died in 1822.

37. Pathologies noted in the region by Gottschalk and other travellers.

38. Heine is referring to the support that the Prussian royal family gave to associations devoted to converting the Jews. As for the situation of the Jewish community in Prussia, it is worth noting that an edict of 1822 had abolished the civil and political rights of Jews recognized ten years before.

39. Peak of the Andes, in Ecuador, partially ascended by Alexander von Humboldt, who made it famous with his descriptions.

40. Willem Beukelsz of Biervlit, whose "invention" was even celebrated in Latin verses; the poem *De Buckelingi genio* by J.B.G. Camberlyn d'Amougies appeared in 1827.

41. The social class of miners had particular practices, customs, and rituals, linked to an activity which, on the threshold of the industrial era, seemed to represent an initiation into the mysteries of nature, and at the same time, to their profanation. From this stems the myth of the mines in Romantic poetry with Novalis, Tieck, Brentano, and E.T.A. Hoffmann. In Heine's description, instead, there is a lack of

magical or symbolic aspects, an abundance of realistic details, and a prevailing objective tone.

42. Marie-Joseph Motier de Lafayette (1757–1834), who had fought for United States independence, made a long trip to America in 1824–25 and was greeted everywhere with enthusiasm and affection.

43. The storm took Heine by surprise in August 1823, during the passage from Cuxhaven to Helgoland; this experience was recorded in his letters, in *Heimkehr*, and provided material for the *Nordsee* lyric cycles.

44. The youngest son of the King George III of England, Adolphus Frederick, Duke of Cambridge, was Governor General of Hannover from 1816.

45. The figure of the faithful Eckart entered the tradition of German heroic legend as a model for an unshakable spirit of loyalty toward his own lord. In the nineteenth century, Ludwig Tieck, among others, made use of this subject in the tale *Faithful Eckart and Tannhäuser* (1799), in which the Burgundian duke has the children of his vassal put to death, and in spite of this, the latter remains faithful to him.

46. All of these are themes taken from the Grimm brothers' fairytales. The influence that fairytales, and in general the tradition of German folk poetry, exerted on Heine is expressed here in a reflexive and analytical tone.

47. A reference to Friedrich Boutewerk (1766–1828), professor of aesthetics at Göttingen from 1802. Heine had read his history of eloquence and probably had attended his lectures.

48. The author of *Schlemihl* had in fact undertaken a journey through the Harz at the same time. Heine had met and been impressed by him in Berlin.

49. In the tenth century, at the time of the Saxon emperors, Goslar was the capital of the Holy Roman Empire's Germanic nation.

50. One might link this unclear expression to Heine's claims in several letters from that period that German was a torturous language.

51. The cathedral, which dated back to the eleventh century, had been demolished in 1819 because of its instability. The imperial throne was moved to Berlin in 1820 and then returned to Goslar in 1867.

52. A formula of Roman rhetoric connected to judicial discourse in order to guarantee the completeness of an oral argumentation or writing of a theme.

53. Perhaps Heine had in mind the play *Die Gründung Prags* (*The Foundation of Prague,* 1815) by Clemens Brentano, where in fact a legend from Carniola is mentioned,where the man on the moon is called Clothair.

54. A pro-government newspaper, and thus opposed by liberals as reactionary, published in Vienna from 1810 to 1832.

55. Saul Ascher (1767–1822) was a Jewish bookseller and philosopher from Berlin. A scholar of Kant and advocate of enlightened Judaism, he belonged—like Heine, Leopold Zunz, the founder of Hebrew studies, and Eduard Gans—to the "Verein für Kultur und Wissenschaft der Juden." He was in fact the author of numerous essays and pamphlets: the one on Christianity which the text alludes to below is *Ansichten von dem künftigen Schicksale des Christentums* of 1819.

56. The short story *Das warnende Gespenst* (*The Warning Spirit*) published in the *Deutsche Erzählungen* (*German Narrations*) in 1815 by Karl August Varnhagen von Ense (1785–1858). This is a quotation that repays a debt of friendship and esteem to Varnhagen and especially to his Jewish wife, Rahel Levin (1771–1833).

57. This refers to the chapter *Von dem Grunde der Untersheidung aller Gegenstände überhaupt in Phaenomena und Noumena* (*On the Basis of Distinction between Objects in Phenomena and Noumena*).

58. In the *Book of Songs* with the title *Idyll on the Mountains*.

59. See Lessing, *Nathan the Wise*, the last verse of Act II: "Der wahre Bettler ist / Doch einzig und allein der wahre König" (the true beggar is also the only true king).

60. In the *Book of Songs* with the title *Der Hirtenknabe* (*The Shepherd Boy*).

61. According to an ancient legend (which Heine probably knew from the corresponding *Volksbuch* and Ludwig Tieck's play of 1800), Genoveva of Bramante, unjustly accused of adultery, took refuge in a forest and there gave birth to her son Schmerzenreich ("abounding in sorrow"), who was nursed by a doe.

62. That wicked spirits used masses of granite to play ball is a very frequent theme in sagas and legends. Heine might have known it from the *Deutsche Sagen* (*German Sagas*) published by the Grimms in 1816.

63. Friedrich August Moritz Retsch (1779–1857) was a painter from Dresden. He executed a series of illustrations for the edition of Goethe's *Faust* published by Cotta in 1816.

64. Heine's two youthful tragedies; published in 1823, they had little success.

65. In the scene "Night-Open Country" in Goethe's *Faust*, also Faust and Mephistopheles, having run into a band of witches, spur their black horses. It seems certain that in this period Heine had it in mind to work over the Faust material, but this idea took shape only in 1851, with the parody in the ballet *Doctor Faust*.

66. Heine takes this quotation from the *Rheinweinlied* by Matthias Claudius (1740–1815).

67. The same in which Faust and Mephistopheles wander in *Faust I*.

68. To be exact, the letter of October 3, 1779 from the *Briefe aus der Schweiz* (*Letters from Switzerland*) by Goethe.

69. The novel had been republished in the Jubilee edition of Goethe in 1825, and for a short while it was again fashionable to read it.

70. Heine frequented her salon in Berlin. The baroness, who had actually translated Byron and Scott, encouraged Heine's poetic talent by calling him "the German Byron."

71. The English poet is one of the young Heine's models, whom he studied, imitated, translated, and soon distanced himself from.

72. Leland's translation presents here the following, additional passage: "and in the spirit we found ourselves again in our learned Siberia, where refinement is carried to such an extent that bears are 'bound by many ties' in the taverns, and sables wish the hunter good evening."

73. Extremely severe measures had been taken against the liberal students in Halle. See also *Heimkehr, LXXXIV* in the *Book of Songs*.

74. Christian Gottfried Schütz (1747–1833), a classical philologist at the University of Halle, had been the object of student protests.

75. A double target of satire: the undergraduates who joined together to found the so-called "beer states" and the despotic courts of German particularism.

76. Probably expelled from a university center due to suspicions of "demagogic activities"—that is, of taking part in the *Burschenschaft* banned by law.

77. A well-known Berlin gathering spot.

78. From the *Death of Wallenstein* by Friedrich Schiller, Act II, Scene 2, line 4537.

79. Karl Moritz von Brühl, Superintendent of the Royal Theater from 1815 to 1828, a fanatic for historical correctness in staging.

80. Lazarus Gumpel, a Jewish banker: he was probably the Marquis Gumpelino in Heine's *Baths of Lucca*.

81. In Schiller's *Mary Stuart*.

82. A professor of zoology who in those years was setting up the Berlin zoological gardens.

83. From one of the best-known dramatic hodge-podges, with the same title, by August Kotzebue (1761–1819).

84. Gaspare Spontini had been greeted with great acclaim in Berlin, where he was court choir master and the opera's musical director from 1820.

85. Michel François Hoguet, star dancer for the Berlin Opera.

86. Paul Ferdinand Friedrich Buchholz (1768–1842), historian and publisher of historical-political journals.

87. These were also ballerinas at the Berlin theater.

88. In 1818, the Swiss master pastry chef Giavanoli inaugurated the first pastry shop in Berlin.

89. From the second chapter of *Don Quixote*, one of Heine's favorite books.

90. After his victory over Napoleon (1814), the Field Marshall G.L. Blücher had become an idol to Teuton-crazed students—here a target of Heine's caricaturing.

91. A proposal endorsed by numerous groups inspired by liberal nationalism after the fall of the Germanic Holy Roman Empire.

92. It was during these years that research on the Germanic tribes and their ancient virtues—the ancient Germanic freedom already praised by Tacitus—intensified, and the figure of Hermann (or Arminius) attracted the interest of writers: a prime example is *Arminius' Battle* by Heinrich von Kleist (1809, posthumous edition 1821).

93. Friedrich Ludwig Jahn, the founder of several patriotic gymnastic associations from 1811 on, subsequently absorbed in part by the *Burschenschaften*. He provided a sort of paramilitary regimentation to young Germans anxious for revenge after the defeat at Jena and French occupation (and inflamed by Fichte's *Discourses to the German Nation*).

94. Today Wilhelm Müller (1794–1827) is remembered for his collection of *Lieder* (1821) that constituted the texts for Franz Schubert's lieder cycles *Die schöne Müllerin* and *Die Winterreise*. It must be mentioned, however, that this author of famous lieder in a popular vein was also the author of political poems for the Greek struggle for independence against the Turks, which transfigured the poet's own experiences in the wars against Napoleon.

    Friedrich Rückert (1788–1866) had published in 1816 the *Geharnischte Sonette* (*Sonnets in Armor*), patriotic, anti-Napoleonic poems that made him very popular amongst students.

    Ludwig Uhland (1787–1862) had published his first and most successful volume of poetry in 1815. His skill as a jurist led him to take sides in 1818 for the preservation of ancient common law in Württemberg.

95. The author of a collection of student, patriotic, folk, and military lieder, Albert Gottlieb Methfessel (1785–1869) lived in Hamburg since 1823 as a voice teacher and composer. Heine knew him and wrote a review of his *Liederbuch* in November 1823.

96. The then famous attack on the *Vaterslandlied* (1812) by Ernst Moritz Arndt (1769–1860). A professor of German history, he was relieved of his teaching duties in Bonn (where Heine frequented

him) for his support of the liberal national movement. He was the best-known source of inspiration for anti-Napoleonic propaganda, a tireless advocate of love for the German fatherland in his numerous pamphlets and, above all, in his very popular works of patriotic poetry.

97. Perhaps the best-known of fate tragedies by Adolf Müllner (1813).

98. A small organ used in the XV and XVI centuries.

99. Reference to a *Volkslied* contained in the collection by Herder and then in *The Boy's Magic Horn*; perhaps there is an ironic allusion to Goethe, who greatly admired that song.

100. Parody of the paratactic style and the suggestive metaphors of the poems of Ossian, and from this an indirect parody of *Werther* as well as the trivializations of Ossianic moods during the Restoration.

101. A translation from Ossian's hymn *Dar-thula*.

102. Word-by-word repetition of Ossian's *Berrathon* in the translation inserted by Goethe to highlight Werther and Lotte's last encounter.

103. The lex Falcidia of 44 B.C. limited the freedom of a testator, obliging him to set aside a part of his wealth for his legitimate heirs.

104. A specialist of the history of law, Eduard Gans (1798–1839) had published in 1824 *Erbrecht in weltgeschichtlicher Entwicklung (The Law of Succession in World History)*. A Jew like Heine, Gans headed the "Verein für Kultur und Wissenschaft der Juden," an association of young Jewish intellectuals who studied the history of Judaism in order to reform it and break down the barriers that separated Jews and Christians. It was Gans who introduced Heine to the "Verein" and, above all, indicated to him a conception of law alternative to that of the Historical School. As he gained access to an academic career, Gans closed his "Verein" experience, preceding Heine on the way to baptism.

105. The jurist Johann Friedrich Ludwig Göschen (1797–1858), who was the director, with Savigny, of the official journal of the Historical School.

106. Christian Friedrich Elvers (1791–1858), a jurist linked to the Historical School, who taught law at Göttingen.

107. The first words of Chapter 2 in the Lex Falcidia.

108. The most ancient collection of Roman laws

109. Later entitled *Auf dem Brocken* (*On the Brocken*).

110. The Persian nightingale that makes its appearance in nineteenth-century German letters through Goethe's *Westöstlicher Divan* (1819) and Friedrich Rückert's collection *Östlichen Rosen* (1822).

111. The reference is more likely to Sir William Congreve, the English physicist and artillery general who invented incendiary missiles, than to the erotic comedies of William Congreve (1670–1729).

112. Made famous in Germany by Goethe's description of it in his *Italian Journey*.

113. Clauren is the pseudonym of Carl Gottlieb Samuel Heun, author at that time of pulp romance novels.

114. Theophrastus Bombast of Hohenhein (Paracelsus), to whom Heine erroneously ascribed a theory of smell attributable instead to Theophrastus of Lesbos, a pupil of Plato.

115. The "Ilse" in the *Book of Songs*, where the water fairy is a benevolent and protective Heine's (and others') version of Lorelei. The poem combines typical Romantic themes for a humorous-pragmatic finale.

116. See Kant, in the *Critique of Judgment*.

117. The idea of Romanticism and Hegel, as was later the case in *Ideen. Das Buch Le Grand* (*Ideas: The Book Le Grand*), mocked and reduced to inconclusive ideology.

118. The tomb of Till Eulenspiegel, the jester, is supposedly located at Mölln, near Lübeck.

119. Probably the not-at-all famous Theodor Winkler.

120. In 1824 Ludwig Ferdinand Niemann published the guidebook to the Harz which Heine refers to.

121. Perhaps the *Chronik der Sassen* (*Chronicle of the Saxons*) of 1492 or the *Liber cronicarum* by Hartmann Schedel (1493), or one of the numerous illustrated chronicles which Heine used to leaf through at that time, in search of sources for his *Rabbi of Bacherach*.

122. Allusion to Heine's Lutheran baptism celebrated in great secret, shortly before his graduation, on June 28, 1825: it was a formal act, very common among the emancipated Jews who were then banned by the Prussian government from public offices. Heine, however, did not take the event for granted: perhaps because it was difficult for him to believe at the time that he could thus resolve his own double, contradictory identity as a Jew and as a German.

123. Georg Sartorius (1765–1828) taught political history at Göttingen. Heine attended his lectures and frequented his home, holding him in great esteem for his intellectual and political open-mindedness.

124. Heine's version of Winckelmann's famous definition of Greek beauty.

125. From the countryside around Hamburg known for its produce.

126. The promenade in Hamburg.

127. They are the flowers peopling the *Book of Songs*.

THE HARZ JOURNEY

was printed and bound in April 1995 by TPM
of Padua, Italy. The text was set and designed
by Paolo Barlera on Adobe ten- and nine-point
Simoncini Garamond and ten-point Stempel
Garamond typefaces.

Marsilio Classics

Amerigo Vespucci, *Letters From A New World*
Denis Diderot, *The Indiscreet Jewels*
Jacques Cazotte, *The Devil in Love*
Carlo Goldoni, *The Holiday Trilogy*
Lauro Martines, *An Italian Renaissance Sextet*
Heinrich Heine, *The Harz Journey*
Antonio Pigafetta, *The First Voyage Around the World*

Forthcoming

Carlo Goldoni, *The Coffee House*
Ralph Waldo Emerson, *Representative Men*
Cesare Beccaria, *On Crimes and Punishments*